Otto Lerbinger Boston University

Nathaniel H. Sperber Consultant

KEY TO THE EXECUTIVE HEAD

ADDISON-WESLEY PUBLISHING COMPANY
Reading, Massachusetts · Menlo Park, California
London · Amsterdam · Don Mills, Ontario · Sydney

ISBN 0-201-04258-4
ABCDEFGHIJ-CO-7987654

Contents

Introduction

Executive insulation is a luxury of the past. No longer can the company chairman or president cloister himself in the hushed isolation of the executive suite and dispassionately view the world. Nor can he remain obscured behind a one-way mirror, seeing and manipulating his subjects while remaining hidden from view.

These subjects—constituents in growing numbers who are affected by corporate decisions—seek participation and power. They see the chief executive as the dominant target—the person at the top of the corporate power structure and, along with government, at the summit of national power. Disillusioned with Congress, union officials, and other traditional leaders, people have turned to social activists—men like Ralph Nader, Barry Commoner, and John Banzhaf who, together with their consumerism, environmental, and other groups, are seen as the challengers of corporate power.

Flushed from behind protective office walls, the chief executive is now the chief actor in a theatre-in-the-round. He has no backdrop to lean on, no big gold curtain for concealment, no wings to dodge into. The chief executive is totally exposed.

Omniconfrontation describes this new setting:

- Upon arriving at work, the chief executive may find a band of black leaders and churchmen protesting the company's operation of a mine in Namibia.

1

- A newspaper clipping on the executive's desk states that the head of a South American subsidiary has been kidnapped and that a ransom of $15 million is demanded.

- On the schedule for the day is a meeting with the corporate secretary to discuss three proxy proposals, submitted by the Project on Corporate Social Responsibility, asking for a broadening of the board membership. This group also wants more disclosure on pollution-abatement measures and minority efforts and a termination of operations in South Africa.

- The phone rings; Jack Anderson is on the line wanting to know about a $100,000 political contribution allegedly made by the company to a political candidate.

- At noon, the chief executive is due at the Economic Club to deliver a luncheon speech on "Balancing Ecology with Economic Growth."

All these events may not happen in a single morning, but these and many others do occur in a period of a month or year. The chief executive is sought out by both traditional and new claimants, petitioners, supplicants, and accusers.

Studies have shown that even before the age of confrontation, chief executives spent between two-thirds and nine-tenths of their time in contact with other people, either inside or outside their companies. About 35 percent of their time is specifically spent on the "representation" function. This includes preparation for meetings, travel time, business luncheons, and contacts with various types of people—government officials, suppliers, reports, trade union officials, and others. *Business Week*'s May 4, 1974, special issue on "The Chief Executive Officer" quotes Alonzo L. McDonald, Jr., managing partner of McKinsey & Co. as saying, "Just a few years ago the CEO of a big company spent 10% of his time on external matters. . . . Today the figure is generally 40%."

In a hostile business climate, however, chief executives must now spend more time dealing with outside groups. These groups have multiplied and have sharpened their tactics. One directory of environmental groups lists no fewer than 45,000.

Included are historical ones, such as the Sierra Club, the Wilderness Society, and the National Audubon Society, as well as new ones, such as Friends of the Earth and a public-interest legal group, the Environmental Defense Fund. There are corporate-responsibility organizations, activist church groups, such as the National Council of Churches and its Corporate Information Center, student groups, consumerism groups, minority militants, and a bewildering variety of other social-action groups.

The tactics they use to gain top-level attention are the familiar ones borrowed from trade unions—strikes, pickets, and boycotts—as well as those developed in the civil rights movement—demonstrations, mass meetings, marches, and sit-ins. In addition to class-action suits and other legal remedies increasingly used by consumer and environmental groups, there are fires, vandalism and trashing, bombs, and other forms of violence used by radical groups. The most potent tactic, to be discussed later, is the extraordinarily clever use of publicity —expert utilization of both print and electronic media.

What is frightening is the fact that despite the upsurge of activity in the social sector, the vast majority of company presidents and chairmen don't see any need to change their responses. They delude themselves that their corporate structures are profitable and impregnable. The problem, they insist, is merely in maintaining law and order and in educating the public.

Like the architects of modern office buildings, they claim that their structures are fireproof. When this delusion goes up in smoke—as fires in modern structures in New Orleans, São Paulo, and Tokyo have proved—they install sprinklers and call it an early-warning system. But, as with the generals and admirals at Pearl Harbor who couldn't be reached or whose preconceptions couldn't be changed when the radarman warned of an attack, the results are the same. Most chief executives still believe that the early-warning signals will go away or prove to be exaggerated.

Whether we examine *Business Week, Fortune,* the *Wall Street Journal,* or the spate of books on business and society, there is agreement on a basic theme: the corporation is under siege as never before. Most writers believe that steady, incremental changes will preserve our corporate and economic systems. A few believe that drastic changes are the only remedy.

In our view, corporate chief executives hold the key to the outcome. They can preserve the basic strengths of our system by doing two things. First, they must become public figures, unafraid to speak out on public issues that affect their corporations or the public they serve; they must be willing to enter a "fourth dimension," as we shall discuss in Part III. Second, they must give life and meaning to the rhetoric that a corporation is not only an economic institution, but a social and political one as well. Part III, dealing with hard-core accountability, discusses the implications of this broader view of the modern corporation's responsibilities.

Because we see the chief executives of the country's leading corporations as prime movers in effecting change, we have sought to learn more about them. A review of the literature shows that pitifully little is known about these figures in the contemporary world. The chief executives remain an enigma shrouded in stereotypes and melded with their corporate images. They are no longer the individualists their predecessors were. Occasionally, a Harold Geneen, Henry Ford, II, or David Rockefeller makes the front pages or television screens, but to the average American these men are either obscure and inscrutable or platitudinous.

To penetrate the fog of ignorance surrounding this country's chief executives, we decided on a novel approach—to ask corporate public relations directors to describe their chief executives. It's obvious that a public relations director knows more about the public side of a company president or chairman than any other staff member does. Public relations directors —sometimes called "alter egos"—help chief executives project themselves and their ideas to the public. Thus, we feel confident in saying that PR directors are qualified to observe the following: the impression chief executives make in public, how well they express themselves, what public-policy issues are uppermost in their minds, how truthful they are, how they react to threatening situations, and what their social values are.

Questionnaires were mailed beginning in November 1973 to all known public relations directors of the Fortune 500 corporations and the second 500 largest industrial corporations. A second mailing went to 100 leading public relations consulting firms, asking them to respond on the basis of the chief executive they knew best among their prestigious clients. Of 1100 questionnaires sent, 238 were returned—a 22 percent return, which is outstanding for a survey as sensitive as this. The survey questionnaire, called "A PR View of the Company President," appears in Chapter 13, along with a tabulation of results. Findings and interpretations appear throughout the book. Although the respondents are, and must remain, anonymous, they speak for the nation's leading corporations.

I
CONFRONTATION

1
The chief executive goes public

The nature of the job requires a company president or chairman to operate both inside and outside his company. He is a boundary-spanner who relates the one to the other. But the ratio of this attention has varied with historical periods of business growth. In the past, when technological and production problems were greatest, the chief executive was primarily an inside person. In more recent years, the chief executive has tried to adapt, and shuttle between, the financial and marketing segments of the outside, but he has still remained mainly an inside-oriented person. Now and in the future, however, the chief executive has no choice but to focus on outside pressures. The president must go public.

The reasons for this shift in orientation have already been reviewed. They add up to the inescapable fact that confidence in big corporations—along with other "establishment" institutions—is probably the lowest in history. Opinion Research Corporation studies show that from 1965 to 1972, the share of the American public expressing low approval for business climbed from 47 percent to a clear-cut majority of 60 percent. Three-quarters of the American public believes that corporations have grown too powerful for the good of the country (*Business Week*, May 4, 1974). The loss in support comes from Republicans, professionals, managers, and the affluent, as well as Democrats, lower occupational groups, and the poor.

Management has to face up to the fact that it lives in an open society that has become disenchanted with the way business operates. There is an *a priori* presumption of guilt. From bitter experience, most chief executives know that when the barometer of public opinion stubbornly sticks to a low reading long enough, it indicates a vacuum, and the winds of government come rushing in. To avoid this inevitable consequence of inaction, they know that something must be done.

But the something too many executives have done typifies not the president in public but the president in private. Fearing unfavorable publicity, chief executives avoid direct confrontation with hostile groups and divisive issues. Using a legal approach, they question the legitimacy of claims made or the groups making them. Using their public relations staffs, they insist that the public be informed and educated as to the true facts and the "American Way." Although they may do all this in good faith, they don't realize that they're actually insensitive to the real issues at stake. Nor do they recognize their own behavior as being defensive and actually counterproductive.

Chief executives still like to believe that competitive forces in the marketplace safeguard the public interest, even as they buy out or merge with their competitors. And when they're accused of having amassed too much power, they'll even forget their ideological differences with Kenneth Galbraith and borrow his theory of countervailing power—that the public interest is protected because business power is offset by other giant concentrations of power, such as the unions.

If the mechanisms of competition and countervailing power really worked, the barometer of public opinion would always read "fair." Telling people that their perceptions and attitudes are wrong doesn't change the forecast of "stormy." The underlying causes of the symptoms of discontent must be identified. Then solutions must be worked out.

It is the working out of these solutions that most requires the chief executive to go public. Increasingly, no single institution in society—be it government, nonprofit organizations, or business—has the information, knowledge, and resources to do it alone. Many problems, such as inflation and the energy shortage, are national and international in scope. Other problems, such as environmental improvements, cut across city, state, regional, and international boundaries. Problems of law and order, crime, and drugs require economic, social, and political solutions—not segmented ones, but joint, integrated approaches.

By training and experience, the chief executive has one important qualification for work in the public sphere: he is a generalist. Within his own company he has learned to listen to the narrow recommendations of his specialized staff units and then to decide, from a broad, companywide perspective, what policy or action is most profitable. His decisions stick because the legitimacy of his authority is more or less unquestioned (but now, even that premise is being challenged).

The president in public must extend his orientation to a less self-centered view of what the public interest is. What's good for GM is not always good for the country, as "Engine" Charlie Wilson got tired of hearing. The undisputed authority of a company chief executive to decide ultimately what's best for his company simply doesn't extend to his participation in the public sphere. He has to stop thinking that everybody else is wrong and that only he is right. Nobody has a crystal ball that reveals what's in the balanced best interests of all.

An arsenal of techniques for resolving social conflict is needed to arrive at equitable and workable solutions. The single most critical skill, however, is sensitivity to the opinions of the public. The chief executive is traditionally adept at understanding rational facts and logical arguments. Our survey certainly underscores his ability to hear and absorb oral presentations and to understand written materials (see Chapter 4). But his strength in cognitive matters seems to have drained him of an ability to understand the feelings of others or the vagaries of public opinion. According to one study, *Corporate Policies and Public Attitudes* by Robert W. Miller, most chief executive officers don't even seem to have any sense of certainty as to what the public actually thinks about their own companies and how public attitudes can be measured and defined. Much less is probably known about attitudes toward public issues and public groups.

To test chief executives' responsiveness to public opinion and public pressures, our survey explored three forms of behavior: their availability to their public relations directors, the kinds of outside inquiries they prefer to handle themselves, and the way they react to threatening situations.

Public relations today deals not only with communications with a company's various publics, but also with attempts to resolve social conflicts. For this reason, a public relations director's ready access to the chief executive is a sign that public opinion and attention to the sociopolitical environment get high priority.

We found that 59 percent of the public relations directors report directly to the president or chairman. Thirty-nine percent do not report directly to the top, but to a group vice-president, a vice-chairman, or some other intermediary. Organizational reporting lines are sometimes shortened, for some comments indicate that "in practice" or "depending on the subject," the public relations director does see the chief executive directly. Except for a minority of companies in which the chief executive insulates himself from public relations and the outside pressures it symbolizes, most companies show that their antennae are out.

But public relations considerations are not of primary concern in the executive suite, as suggested by the small percentage of public relations directors who think that they have a chance of becoming president of the company. As shown below, 61 percent believe that they have absolutely no chance, and only 15 percent think that they have an average or above average chance.

Facts gathered by *Public Relations News* indicate that some public relations directors do make it to the top. Between

Excellent	1.7
Better than average	4.6
Average	8.8
Lower than average	21.4
None	60.9
No answer or other	2.5

1966 and 1973, the following were named to the position of chairman or president of companies: J. Stanford Smith, International Paper Company; Charles O. Peyton, Exxon International; Edwin D. Dodd, Owens-Illinois; William J. Cadigan, Massachusetts Electric Co.; C. Edward Utermohle, Jr., Baltimore Gas & Electric; Harold V. Gleason, Franklin National Bank; Eugene F. Jannuzi, Moltrup Steel. A little-known fact is that James M. Roche, former chairman of General Motors, had been public relations director of Buick.

Anyone familiar with the operation of large, formal organizations can readily understand why the chief executive wishes to ignore the pesty new groups. Bureaucracies are wondrous machines that get complicated tasks performed, sometimes highly efficiently. But each specialist wears blinders and assiduously avoids situations which might disrupt carefully worked-out routines. For the chief executive, who is no different from these specialists, the ability to orchestrate the various company units depends on the predictability of their performance and the degree to which he is insulated from outside pressures. The greater the chief executive's autonomy, the more he can maintain control.

Public relations departments have done an excellent job of providing stability and predictability in relationships with the government and the traditional social sector of society—church, veterans groups, social agencies, museums, symphony associations, etc. Every alert company conducts some kind of "public relations audit," listing all the important internal and external publics with which it has dealings or which could affect its welfare. Various forms of "fever charts," similar to those used by American presidents to track their popularity, have also been kept. Unfavorable showings or drastic drops in attitudes toward the corporation, its management, or products receive quick, remedial attention.

But by the mid-1960s more was required than the typical remedial actions of improved communications, some visibility in the social responsibility area, and internal reorganization. Racial disorders in 1967 drew attention to social inequities and more particularly to the hard-core unemployed, who were culturally and emotionally disbarred from the labor market. Well-intentioned programs by government and business helped some. But it was soon evident that this and the related problem of growing welfare rolls were too big for anything but such drastic measures as a guaranteed annual wage.

Campus disorders, triggered mainly by protests against the Vietnam war, spread the social infection. Government was one victim. The Institute for Social Research warned that distrust of government grew so alarmingly from 1964 to 1972 that "continued growth of this distrust could create a generation of cynical Americans and plunge this country into a cycle of discontent." Blacks' trust in government deteriorated four times as rapidly as that of whites. Business was implicated in this study in that one of the five measures used asked whether the government in Washington is pretty much run by a few big interests looking out for themselves or for the benefit of all the people.

Other studies focused on business even more. A survey commissioned by CBS to study the generation gap showed that 34 percent of college students and 21 percent of noncollege youth wanted "fundamental reform" of big business. The study concluded, however, that young people were willing to work within the system, for 52 percent were satisfied with "moderate change of big business." A more pointed survey, *Criticism of Business*, conducted by General Electric in 1970 and 1971, showed a surprisingly large minority of college students who said that "all" or "most" businesses are guilty of some of the offenses charged by campus radicals. For example, to the statement "Business will not do anything in the public interest if it reduces their profits," the responses in 1971 were: 5 percent, "all"; 33 percent, "most"; 51 percent, "some"; and only 10 percent, "none."

No wonder that top management was alarmed and that crisis management became a normal part of business. We wondered, however, how the chief executives of the nation's leading corporations typically reacted to threatening situations. In Question 7 we listed eight situations and a six-item crisis reaction scale: (1) "treats as major crisis," (2) "shows extreme concern," (3) "becomes totally preoccupied," (4) "applies standard operating procedure," (5) "shrugs off to subordinates," and (6) "treats casually." The gradations range from strong to weak.

Figure 1 shows the number of chief executives who considered each of the eight situations extremely threatening. Only the first two reactions—"treats as major crisis" and "shows extreme concern"—were used for this measurement. The third intense reaction—"becomes totally preoccupied"—was omitted because it was rarely checked off.

Condemnation by a governmental agency—the FTC, FDA, SEC, etc.—frightened the chief executive the most. Twenty percent would treat it as a major crisis, and an additional 41 percent would show extreme concern. And why not? When the legitimacy of an entire industry is threatened, as the cigarette industry was with the Surgeon General's announcement that there was a link between cigarette smoking and cancer, then everything is at stake and nothing should command greater attention. If survival is not the issue, profits are; they can be severely crippled when the safety of such foods as cyclamates and cranberries is questioned.

Lesser forms of condemnation are also anxiety-producing, as Continental Baking Co. discovered when it was accused of deceptive advertising by the FTC. These situations create an atmosphere of uncertainty and cause unfavorable publicity. The financial community and others might infer that the management of the company is not too sharp.

Striking at the heart of the executive's personal survival and his control of the corporation are the "acquisition or tender offer" and "proxy fight"—the second and third most threatening situations. As shown in Fig. 1, the percentage of executives who respond with severe reactions is 53 percent and 52 percent, respectively.

More significant is that the portion of these percentages accounted for by the most extreme reaction—treating as a major crisis—is highest of the eight situations. On this basis, a proxy fight is seen as more threatening than an acquisition or tender offer, for the former is treated as a major crisis by 38 percent of the executives, compared to 30 percent for the latter.

Table 1 presents this fact in comparison to the eight threatening situations by showing the most typical executive reaction (typical is defined as the reaction to each situation re-

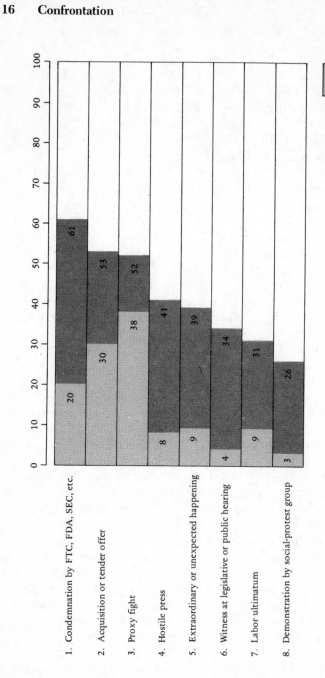

FIG. 1. Percentage of chief executives who treat situation as a major crisis or show extreme concern.

ceiving the highest percentage, i.e., the statistical mode). Only
these two personal survival issues—the acquisition or tender
offer and proxy fight—are treated as a major crisis. Even "condemnation by FTC, FDA, SEC, etc." shows the most typical
reaction to be a degree less severe, namely, to show extreme
concern.

That these corporate survival issues are reacted to most
strongly is supported by another fact. Table 1 shows the most
typical reaction to the eight situations (typical is defined as the
reaction mentioned most frequently, i.e., the statistical mode).

TABLE 1.
MOST TYPICAL REACTION TO SITUATIONS

	Treats as major crisis	Shows extreme concern	Applies SOP
Condemnation by FTC, FDA, SEC, etc.		×	
Acquisition or tender offer	×		
Proxy fight	×		
Hostile press		×	
Extraordinary or unexpected happening			×
Appearing as witness at legislature or public hearing			×
Labor ultimatum			×
Demonstration by social-protest group			×

The fourth and fifth situations that threaten the chief executive the most—as measured by the first two extreme reactions
—are a "hostile press" and an "extraordinary or unexpected
happening." The former ("hostile press") received 41 percent
of the mentions; the latter ("extraordinary happening"), 39 percent. That they run close together is not surprising, since a
hostile press often reports an unfavorable or unsettling event.
However, as shown by the most typical reaction in Table 1,
chief executives show extreme concern with a hostile press, but
simply apply standard operating procedures (SOPs) to an unexpected happening.

A hostile press implies many things. First, it refers to muck-raking and investigative reporting and resultant unwelcome exposure. Not only news stories, but also editorials lash out at business in general, particular industries, e.g., oil, and specific companies, e.g., ITT. The press is also found to be hostile when it serves as a ready vehicle for press releases issued by government agencies. A form of "trial by press release" is illustrated by Federal Trade Commission policies. In the 1960s Jack Anderson could call the FTC a "sepulcher of official secrets" and condemn it as having the worst agency regulations in light of the Freedom of Information Act. In contrast, the FTC now routinely issues press releases on some 23 categories of commission actions and often uses press releases as a club to enforce its wishes without resorting to litigation.

Finally, a hostile press means that the media serve as an all-too-willing publicist for social-action groups. Theirs is a symbiotic relationship, for the newsworthy events needed by the media are consciously provided by the activists. By staging events that would be out of bounds for corporate publicists, activists manage to make the front pages of newspapers and the evening television news.

In California a group of college students dug a ditch and actually buried a new car to dramatize the need to reduce auto emissions. Protesters against the Vietnam war organized mass meetings, marches, demonstrations, and sit-ins. Housewives boycotted lettuce, grapes, meat. Mothers and grandmothers chained themselves to trees to stop highway-building bulldozers. Ministers bought shares of stock in order to attend stockholder meetings and ask embarrassing questions about a host of subjects: minority employment, military contracting, political contributions, operations in South Africa, to name but a few of the more common ones.

What the young, television generation knows intuitively from thousands of hours of exposure has been put to practice —something novel, disruptive, and violent captures attention; something huge, loud, moving, and highly photogenic is sought out by the media; individualized human interest stuff is the editor's notion of what the public wants to see, hear, and read—

and he has been right many more times than he has been wrong.

Chief executives naturally feel that the media are biased against them. Surveys have shown that the majority of the newsmen and television commentators hold liberal views. The argument is made that although an attempt at objectivity might succeed with a big news story, it is impossible to maintain it on a day-in, day-out basis. No wonder, then, that the typical response of the chief executive to a hostile press is to show extreme concern.

The final three threatening situations—"demonstrations by social protest groups," "appearance as a witness at a legislative or public hearing," and receipt of a "labor ultimatum"—are reacted to in a milder fashion. Here, the chief executive's most typical reaction is to apply standard operating procedures. These situations can be anticipated and are predictable or routine. Thus, they can be coped with and to some extent controlled. Contingency plans can be prepared for protests, executives can be coached for hearings, and tried and proven tactics can be applied to labor relations. SOPs, contingency plans, and other routines are invaluable as ways of avoiding panic and reducing anxiety. But they work best in a relatively stable environment, not in the age of discontinuities as described by Peter Drucker.

The danger of trying to fit old solutions to new problems is illustrated by Eastman Kodak's experience with FIGHT, a black group in Rochester. It demanded that Eastman Kodak train some 500 to 600 blacks. The company's response was to offer the old training program on an "expanded" basis. In a letter to the president of FIGHT, Kodak's president, W. S. Vaughn, said: "We are not in a position to establish any statistical objective or quota for any special training programs which we undertake. Our ability to hire a person at Kodak depends first on the existence of a job opening and, second, on the availability of a person qualified to fill that opening." Kodak did not want to make any commitments, nor did it want to surrender any of its prerogatives in selecting trainees. Words such as "negotiations" and "agreements" were assiduously avoided by nonunion Eastman Kodak.

Establishing new patterns of behavior requires courage. We used to believe that our business leaders possessed that attribute. That's why we called them enterpreneurs, or better yet, innovators. They saw human needs and responded to them; they discerned new technologies and created new products and manufacturing processes; they fearlessly faced up to all problems and found fresh answers.

Today's chief executives must recapture this bold spirit of innovation. Their burden is greater than it was in the past, for they must consider more than economic and technological problems. As if making a profit weren't enough of a challenge, their creativity must be applied to the new and expanding social and political problems.

Word magic will not suffice. Like promissory notes that have come due, assurances given to worried segments of the public that their concerns are not being ignored have already extended beyond their time limits. What is wanted now is performance in all those neglected areas that have caused a loss of confidence in business. Some of these areas, such as job and product satisfaction, lie in the penumbra of economic activities; others lie outside in the sociopolitical environment.

To understand these new problems in full measure, chief executives must lessen the distance between themselves and the people who are affected by their decisions. Like Plato's philosopher-king, they must see, hear, and touch these people in order to understand their problems and their way of thinking. Chief executives cannot rely on computer printouts.

This is the meaning of the age of confrontation: the chief executive has no realistic alternative but to go public.

II
THE PRESIDENTIAL
FOURTH DIMENSION

C.H.W
8.74

2
The seven faces of the president

Janus, the ancient Roman god with two faces, would be hope-
lessly obsolete today. Our new gods—or, if you will, the
chief executives of the companies which control our lives in an
almost unimaginable number of fashions—sport many faces.
They have faces for each of their varying publics and circumstances.

To the union leadership, the president or chief executive
officer (CEO) wears the face of the villainous enemy. To employees, the CEO has the stern look of Jehovah. To the civic
community, the president may appear as either a miser or a
Santa Claus. The list can be as long as you wish.

Now add to that the CEO's "trade" face, which is derived
from the areas of experience and expertise. In the survey conducted among the top 1000 companies, 85 percent of the respondents viewed their chief executives as general managers.
Of course, the stereotype of a general manager is far different
from that of, say, a scientific or technical person. Incidentally,
only 28 percent saw the CEO as a scientific/technical type.

The questionnaire sent to the nation's major corporations
contained, among others, a multiple-choice question dealing
with the backgrounds and strengths of the presidents or chief
executives. In several categories, results were astonishing. Because of the differing orientations, the CEOs appeared as totally different persons. To each of the respondents, the chief

was plainly wearing a different "face." Tabulation of the answers provided the following percentages (total of first four rankings).

General manager	87%
Financial expert	74%
Marketing person	58%
Public relations person	52%
Production manager	41%
Labor/employee consultant	29%
Scientist/technician	28%
Lawyer	24%

Highest of the *first*-place choices was general management (38 percent); lowest was labor/employee consultant (1 percent).

Recently, Avram Goldberg, president and chief executive of Stop & Shop, Inc., the big supermarket chain, commented in an interview that "the greatest danger when you are the head of a company is to surround yourself with people just like you, who think like you and agree with you all the time." The danger seems so obvious that it is astounding that this situation exists at all, let alone prevails in practically every company in the land. In practice, any executive in the three top levels of management who doesn't agree with the boss as to the philosophy, approach, and attitude toward the company, its policies, products, people, etc.—or, if you will, wear a face that's like the boss's—would be wise to up-date his resume. The similarity of philosophy and attitude of the president and top managers —and the concomitant elimination of those who differ—is probably best expressed in Emerson's observation: "Every institution is but the lengthened shadow of a single individual."

In view of this sort of reaction on the part of the chief executive, a question was inserted into the questionnaire which required the respondents to check five out of 22 qualities the chief executive would be most likely to consider pivotal in hiring subordinate executives. It was believed that this would give a relatively accurate description of the CEO's assessment of his own executive qualities.

Percentages of the top five choices were:

Integrity	51%
Acceptance of responsibility	49%
Achievement orientation	44%
Initiative	43%
Reliability	42%

Surprising were some of the qualities that received low desirability scores and thus added unexpected lineaments to the face of the chief executive. For instance, ability to "get along with others" (long considered an operative character quality by the psychology examiners) was broken into three categories. Results indicate that the CEO's face would remain impassive to compatibility.

Getting along with peers	8%
Getting along with superiors	5%
Getting along with subordinates	5%

The quality receiving the lowest score was "curiosity," which to the uninitiated would seem to have been worthy of a higher rating. This recorded a puny 1 percent. "Concentration," which didn't come off much better, received 4 percent. Bunched in the back stretch, with no hope of real consideration, were "prudence" (once the hallmark of a "sound" executive and a trait easily recognizable by a stony-faced board of directors), "boldness," and "ingenuity"—all below 7 percent.

Other qualities and responses in the tabulation were:

Leadership	40%
Loyalty	29%
Drive	28%
Creativity	23%
Enthusiasm	23%
Perception	19%
Communicativeness	13%
Articulateness	10%
Imagination	10%

So much for the precepts inculcated during our early years and passed along by countless generations of Judeo-Christian and Anglo-Saxon ethics. It might almost be worth-while to rewrite the Boy Scout Oath.

Results of this question seem to tell us that the president will seldom wear a quizzical face, or appear as an enthusiast, or even, given a choice, look prudent or bold. Since "integrity" led all other qualities desired in CEOs and potential CEOs, there was a wistful character in the respondents' answers. They wanted their bosses to have an "honest" face. With public confidence in our business leaders dropping to its lowest ebb in decades and with concomitant "presumption of guilt," one must assume that there is a certain naivete in the answers.

Given an extrapolation in time, it would appear that the country's industrial portraits will be dominated by seemingly "honest and ethical" figures who aren't able to communicate very well (and don't give a damn whether or not they do, apparently), who haven't much imagination, enthusiasm, ingenuity, drive, or even the curiosity to speculate on other possibilities.

Now become apparent some of the other "faces" of the chief executives of the companies most vital to our lives. Can these be the same faces that are seen speaking so earnestly and sincerely on TV screens? The ones who reassure us or alarm us via heavily covered press conferences? The same ones who, in full-page advertisements, explain away some of the world's most complicated geopolitical and economical messes with simple, homely logic?

During the formative years of the modern CEO, when the building blocks of characteristics, abilities, qualities, and personalities were being assessed and given priorities as to their importance in the "executive's executive," David McClelland's writings were extremely influential in indicating that achievement orientation was the key factor in the makeup of the successful CEO. Yet "achievement orientation" was only third in the list of qualities sought in potential CEOs. The changes in the ambient executive climate has caused "integrity" to evolve as the leading characteristic. We do want our industry leaders to have integrity; to be honest, to work under some table of ethics—even before we demand of them achievement.

We also find the need for the people who'll be ensconced on the top rung to show a willingness to accept responsibility —to put their heads on the blocks. The day of the "weathercock" deputy seems to have ended. And yet "reliability" comes up with a high score, only one removed from achievement orientation. It's obvious that the presidents want their subordinates and embryonic chief executives to have reliable "faces." Do we then read into that: "someone who can be relied upon to do things as I (the CEO) would"? Certainly, no CEO would consider any executive reliable who did things differently from him.

All the preceding revealed presidential faces resulting from questions that dealt with qualities that were positive, beneficent, pleasant. But what about the negative aspects? How did the respondents react to a question which asked them to delineate by means of 12 traits generally ascribed to CEOs by dissatisfied employees, unhappy consumers, dissident shareholders and others? Not unexpectedly, some 24 percent of all those who returned filled-out questionnaires either refused to answer this question or evaded the unpleasant but relevant facets of their CEOs by answering "none" to all 12 qualities. One can only conclude that these respondents are gullible, unperceptive, or fearful. Thus, the nonanswers are as revealing as though a check mark had been placed next to each of the 12 negative characteristics.

It is no surprise to find that "impatient" was the top critical comment. Almost 33 percent of the respondents found their presidential suite occupied by an individual visibly impatient with subordinates or circumstances. Almost automatically comes the question: "Why does the president have an impatient look?" Is the president just impatient with everyone and everything? Is this impatience caused by all the things with which the chief executive must contend? (There's a temptation for the organization analyst to speculate on the parallelism of impatience and hypertension in chief executives.)

Most likely, we'll find a chief executive who has all the inputs to the scores of daily problems that must be faced and who expects that senior executives (at least, and if they have been selected wisely) will also have the same inputs—and the same priorities. The CEO, who doesn't want to have to draw detailed, reason-why diagrams, becomes abrupt, impatient with those of this executive staff who don't seem to be thinking of the seventh move after king's pawn 4. This impatience is in reality an intolerance of slowness, dullness, lack of acuity. The executive who incurs this reaction and causes the CEO to wear an "impatient" face, even if only a few times, is soon likely to be knocking at a head-hunter's door and being ignored.

In a dead heat with "impatient" for first place in negative executive qualities was "opinionated," which also received 33 percent. There are now two deep creases across the president's forehead. The third facet among the 12 most common critical comments about the CEO was "intolerance of failure," to the tune of 27 percent. Other qualities in this question which were checked off with admirable frankness were:

Close-mouthed	24%
Egotistic	22%
Impersonal/unemotional	19%
Autocratic/dictatorial	18%
Cold/objective	15%
Issue-avoiding	11%
Secretive	11%
Nepotistic	7%
Arrogant	6%
None	7%
No answer	18%

It was no shock to discover that "egotism" ranked so high. Varying degrees of egocentricity are basic ingredients in the success formula not only for industry leaders, but also for politicians, actors, writers, composers, artists, musicians, etc. However, the 4 percent difference between the qualities of "impersonal/unemotional" and "cold/objective" is inexplicable. They would seem to be the same face.

It is significant that in a world and time when the principles of rising expectations and militant consumerism are rampant and communication as a management discipline is deemed important, respondents found CEOs to be "close-mouthed" or "secretive"; it is surprising that "dictatorial" or "arrogant" faces could even be found at all.

In all fairness, it would be untrue to describe the chief executive, whether president or chairman, as a glib actor who facilely dons mask after mask to fit varying occasions. However, to no two publics is the CEO the same person. Most likely, the chief executive responds to differing stimuli with differing reactions, and these responses are not always stereotypical. As delineated by the survey, the chief executive is neither a Dorian Gray nor a latter-day Clark Kent. Rather, the CEO turns out to be totally human—and with the earned luxury of not having to give a damn.

Just when a certain predictability or pattern begins to emerge about the various faces the CEO will wear, holes get shot through them on rechecking the percentages of the answers. The high marks for integrity and acceptance of responsibility are not unexpected, but the responses about prudence are of casual concern. The disregard of the need to get along with others is startlingly new. So, too, is the strength of public relations as an attribute of the president vis-à-vis the relegation of law to the lowest place in total responses.

The importance of the face shown to a specific public on given occasions by any leader is evident globally and throughout time. Consider the lengths to which the individual Oriental, or even entire Eastern countries, will go "to save face." Reread the two and a half columns of closely printed references to "face" and "faces" in Bartlett's quotations and maxims. And finally, in our own era of self-proclaimed sophistication and cynicism, the desirability of having the president sign the full-page advertisement which bears the Karsh-like photograph, is considered vital. So, too, are the time and trouble chief executives take in preparing for their appearances in TV commercials for their companies' policies or products. Consider the advertising campaign of an automobile manufacturer which urges, in neighborly style, that an unhappy buyer need only pick up the telephone to talk—collect, of course—with the president of the company, who will relieve all the consumer's aches and pains almost immediately. Here, we see the president wearing the ombudsman's face.

In sum, the best indication of the pace and pressures of our rapidly changing economy, which in turn shapes the individuals who head our economy, is the need presidents feel for those different faces. Consider, for instance, the Nixonian protocol face vis-à-vis the Oval Office tapes face.

3
The public private

Although he has a barely disguised contempt for most politicians, both high and low, the president or chairman (CEO) is, in fact, a political animal—and, by definition, a highly successful one. All that is needed is a categorical name change. The chief executive officer does not get elected to corporate office in the way that a politician does, after an overt and aggressive campaign. Like the politician, however, the CEO serves only at the will of various constituencies—directors, stockholders, and employees. Should the CEO lose the finely tuned sensitivity to reactions from these constituents, he can indeed lose his post.

The CEO despises politicians generally, believing that every one of them has a price. This cynicism is fortified by the ever-flowing river of demands on the CEO and the company for money donations, subscriptions, overpriced tickets to inedible dinners, and jobs for the politically favored.

On the obverse side, the CEO is continually being reassured by the company's Washington representative (legislative counsel, lobbyist) that favorable legislation is just a matter of contacting the right person at the right time with the right inducement, i.e., the recent confession of a dairy industry representative that he had paid $10,000 to a former cabinet officer to raise price levels (successfully). The CEO also sees the effect of similar actions by competitors or peer groups in industry. Only an imbecile could doubt the dynamic impact on the daily lives of the residents of the United States by such freshly opened cans of catfish bait as (in flamboyant example) the oil lobby or the milk industry. To the chief executive officer, the only consolation is that it's worse in other countries.

There is a certain unease that afflicts many chief executives when they reflect on the political skills, maneuvers, and other activities that have opened the door to the executive suite for them. There seems to be a subconscious recognition of the kinship which exists between them and avowed politicians. Add to this the corporate chiefs' awareness of the burgeoning role of the government in the success—even the survival—of their companies. In many cases, the government—federal or local —is either directly or indirectly a customer of some significance. Corporate chiefs know that willy-nilly, they're in politics. They know, too, that there are no equal partnerships with the government or any political body; they must choose one of three options—join it, give in to it, or suborn it. It would be unnatural for CEOs to slavishly give in. It is repugnant to their egos and the drive which has led them to the top of their chosen organizations. Equally repugnant is the idea (even if it's subconscious) of the outright purchase of that portion of the desired governmental decision. Thus, CEOs are left with only one stream open to them—to dive right in and enjoy the swimming. But generally, most CEOs never doubt that they'll prove superior to the politicians with whom they will have contact.

Two other factors enter into any consideration of the chief executive as a politician. One is a willingness (despite a specious reluctance) to zip down to Washington to "straighten out the mess they've gotten themselves into." Another is a sincere, if often naive, desire to contribute, via his areas of expertise, to the well-being of the country and the people. But most important is the never-articulated preference to have been elected by the general public rather than to have accepted de facto appointment by a small group of directors.

He has the need to know that he's really a "natural leader" rather than governing by the power of position—to hire and fire. The chief executive realizes that successful, long-term governance cannot be achieved by talk alone or by superficialities. The governed want and need accomplishment. The CEO has discovered the poverty of power. Firing people today is not as easy as it used to be, because of unions, public opinion, governmental agency restrictions, etc. He knows that this results in perfunctory performance, and more and more he is forced to heed the dogma: "People do what management *inspects*, not what management *expects*."

Thousands of chief executives have publicly voiced their desire or intention (when mandatory retirement pounds at the door) to take some public job in order to "serve." There's a real inner pressure in this direction, and each CEO has unique ego needs. Each would like to be "drafted" to such an illustrious post, but a post in which the CEO can get the proper respect, will not be pressured any more and, of course, "salary's no object." Concomitant with this desire is a dread of the exposure and the need to practice the flexibility inherent in the politician's credo: "Politics is the art of the practical." Those chief executives who have been successful in such transplants were able to shed their intransigence, to stop being totally dogmatic, to eliminate their computer mentality, i.e., "If you can't count it, it doesn't count." These are traits that cannot be afforded in public life.

Whether they like it or not, the presidents or chairmen, CEOs of the major corporations have indeed become public figures. No longer do they have the luxury of living or working in privacy. The high hedge of isolation which provided the invisibility which was an integral of being the chief executive has been razed by today's public awareness, sophistication, and eagerness for confrontation. Because the general public—consumers and shareholders alike—expect (demand) that industry and its individual corporations be public—in the sense of openness—chief executives must become as exposed and vulnerable as public office holders. And, in the words of Abraham Lincoln, "No man should hold public office unless he's willing to bathe in public opinion."

Presidents and chairmen have new duties and new personality dimensions added to their roles as chief executives. Despite their mutterings and strugglings, they're in the middle of the arena. They're on stage and the spotlights ring them. Consequently, engaging in public affairs is no longer a discretionary choice. It has become a vital business necessity. Some chief executives come easily to the new role; others definitely need guidance and preparation. These individuals must rid themselves of their distaste for public attention. They must take the initiative in activities which bring them favorable exposure. They must be prepared—and their families, too—to stand up under intrusion into their private lives and do it gracefully. If they can do so, they'll find serendipitous benefits for their companies and products.

One result of the private figure becoming a public one has brought dismay to some corporate chiefs and a certain measure of pleasure to others. As the head of a major company, the CEO has shown astuteness and perception in making judgments. And he has been right more times than he's been wrong. The public, then, has a solid expectation that the CEO's judgment on community affairs and knowledge and insight to complex public issues will be equally swift, sure, and superior to their own. The CEO—the respected leader—will be looked to for correct solutions and procedures in national and international affairs. He will become the figure of authority, never to be questioned, for whom even CEOs are subconsciously seeking.

In this evolution, corporate chief executives will find that they are expected to be their own lobbyists. They will find themselves more often in Washington not just to get business or to make deals, but to speak authoritatively for their companies and their industries. The congressmen, senators, and agency heads will listen more attentively than they do to professional lobbyists; they'll react more speedily and directly to the CEO's representations, since they'll be getting unadorned and unencapsulated messages from those who can make the decisions and need not obfuscate. A synergistic effect might well take place at this point; these increasingly public activities may make the CEOs more likely to consider acceptance of high-level governmental office—or even campaign for national office—than was true in the past.

In checking the corporate presidents' or chairmen's in-

volvement in politics, the authors found that not one
respondent's CEO has run for national office. Actually, only
four percent of them went into open competition for state or
local office. However, some 16 percent of the chief executives
have held appointive governmental positions. More often (22
percent) of the chief executives urge their subordinate executives to seek and hold elective or appointive office.

Although 64 percent of the chief executives keep their
political views to themselves, 14 percent felt strongly enough to
get out and campaign actively for specific political candidates.
Obviously, this group is included in the 25 percent who admitted that they aired their views on candidates and preferences.
Often, it seems to be the issue that concerns the chief executive, i.e., tax legislation, employment obligations, restrictive sta-
tutes. This would cause a CEO to back a specific candidate.

But when it came to putting up money instead of participating, the survey revealed that 51 percent gave generously to
either a party or candidate. And, as one respondent differenti-
ated in a marginal note: "Give to a *candidate*, not to an office
holder." In general, donations and support went toward issues
rather than party objectives.

The survey pointed sharply to the changed party preferences on the part of the CEOs. In the past, the stereotypical
president or chairman of a major corporation was invariably
"conservative." In most cases, because of the strong push
toward stability, with an overtone of a small and prudent percentage of annual growth, the chief executive was ultraconserva-
tive. This has changed. There has been an erosion of the
"ultra." The survey shows that although conservatism is still the
single largest political grouping, 41 percent, the alignments
have changed radically. Now 26 percent of the chief executives
are "liberal-conservative," with another 25 percent referred to
as "conservative-liberal." In addition, 6 percent were listed as
"liberals," and .8 percent even went so far as to check off "pro-
gressive." More than 59 percent have defected from the ultra-
conservative category which they chose and in which the
public viewed them.

Although practitioners of the corporate public relations discipline have reason to feel optimistic about a changed future, there's still a substantial way to go before the effects are felt at the operational level. Responses to the questionnaire indicate that chief executives are aware of the changes, but the majority of them are extremely lethargic, if not reluctant, in effecting the departure from the stereotype.

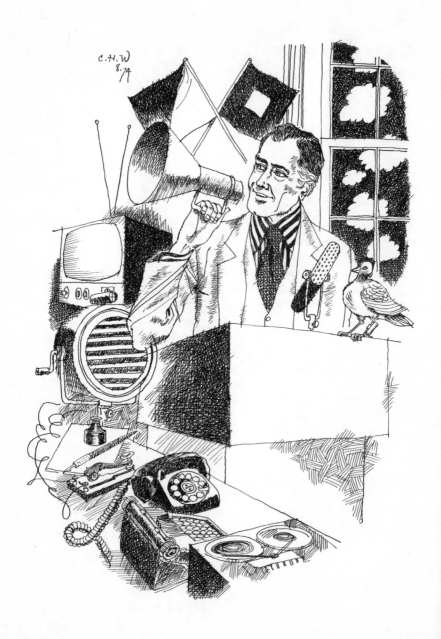

4
Communicator-in-chief

If the present trend continues, the country's corporate chiefs will be the principal, or even the only, spokesmen for their organizations.

This is in sharp contrast to the overlong era we are leaving, when company presidents or chairmen insisted on remaining either mute or totally noncommittal. Their feeling has been that their tasks were to make proper decisions and to administer them profitably—that there was no need to talk to any of their publics. Indeed, in some quarters there was, and still is, an almost scriptural belief that speaking up was likely to be injurious to the company or to the executive. This was abetted by the chief executives' childlike trust in their legal counsels' dictum: "If you don't say anything, you'll have nothing to retract. Anyway, why give the competition a target to shoot at?" This argument has invariably been victorious over the advice given by the chief executive's public relations director: "You've got to make a statement. You must take a positive stand."

Reticence was painfully obvious during the annual stockholder meetings, when only generalities and platitudes flowed suffocatingly over those who owned shares and wanted more detailed information. The birth of the revolt by the dissident shareholder and the accompanying or responsive action by CEOs caused some traumatic labor pains. The day of the semiprivate, 30-minute, "no-discussion" annual meeting is as long gone as 30¢ gasoline. Today, annual meetings can run to marathon lengths. For example, a General Motors meeting with its shareholders (nearly 3000 attending) lasted just under seven hours, and American Telephone & Telegraph Co.'s 85th annual shivaree went on for 305 minutes.

And it's not only dissidents, protest groups, the frustrated fustians, or those who go to enjoy the "circus." More and more stockholders find that they can get answers right from the boss's mouth only at such public and required meetings. Too, as Tom Mullaney, Business News and Financial Editor of the *New York Times* pointed out, meetings are pretty thoroughly covered by the press because it seems that only then can reporters ask questions of chief executives "without having to go through buffers."

The dire need for dialog between the chief executives and their publics is nowhere better expressed than in the handsome success of the yearly publication *Annual Reports of Activities at Corporation Meetings*. These widely read, 300-page books are published by veteran, full-time corporation critics Lewis D. and John J. Gilbert.

There are a few chief executives who welcome these annual organizational orgasms as opportunities—chances to listen as well as to speak. Most CEOs, however, dread them as a breaching of their barriers of isolation, arenas in which they are the Christians and the lions pose rude and crude questions as to their stewardship or probity.

Two corporate meetings point neatly to the two opposing attitudes of chief executives. They are quoted from the 1971 *32nd Annual Reports of Stockholders Activities at Corporation Meetings*. First was what occurred during the four-hour annual meeting of Publicker Industries. "S. S. Neuman, chairman of the board, walked out approximately half way through the session. President A. E. Lang, who took over the meeting, 'stood mute' when pertinent questions were raised concerning executive compensation."

The other case was General Motors, 1971 annual meeting, the last one for James M. Roche, who was retiring. According to the report in *Automotive News*, "Roche stayed at the podium for the entire six hours and fifty-five minutes, replying to hundreds of questions and comments and keeping the meeting moving. As adjournment neared, Lewis D. Gilbert, an annual-meeting regular, told Roche: 'Your conduct of the meeting was as magnificent as it could possibly be.' "

Roche obviously lived up to his obligation as communicator-in-chief. He listened and he spoke. He was effective and he controlled the meeting. As will be seen later in this chapter, the majority of chief executives do not listen; they do not speak effectively; and they do not control meetings.

But presidents or chairmen do not rise to their posts without a real degree of awareness of danger and a recognition that a newer breed of chief executives—highly articulate and actually delighting in being communicative—has moved boldly on stage. There is, too, an awareness that the authoritative mode of "I'll talk, you listen" is being replaced by persuasion. Persuasion seems to get things done. Persuasion can come about only through communication. Without being able to communicate, a chief executive has little chance to persuade. Authority may work some of the time, internally; but never with external publics.

Adding to the pressure on the CEO is the wave of "entitlement," the syndrome of rising expectations that has been cresting. A significant specific of these expectations is a chance to participate—participate personally by questioning the chief executive on policy and plans.

It is no longer enough just to be a good general manager. Now, the chief executive must make an overt personal and corporate commitment—publicly and in person. It's so pragmatic that it's amazing that the change did not come about before. No one—financial reporter, security analyst, or community leader —expects a cogent answer about changes in product lines from the company's attorney; a decision on long-term corporate funding from the marketing vice-president; statements of company policy on continuing thermal pollution of a body of water from the industrial relations manager; or a satisfactory response to questions about union negotiations from the corporate treasurer. No. Only one person in the corporate structure has and can give committing reactions in any and all of these areas on which the company impinges. Since this individual is, by definition, the only generalist in the company, this is the one person that all publics look to for answers. The chief executive—the communicator—is the one person who speaks the one language common to all differing corporate specialists as well as to the various publics. This language is not a specialized jargon, compartmentalized by a single vertical discipline. The CEO, whether president or chairman, is the focal point at which all the beams merge to provide overall enlightenment. And because he makes things coherent, his statements have a laserlike impact.

It is logical that the chief executive be the principal, or perhaps the sole, company spokesman. But it must be more than in title only. There is unfulfilled demand. Only those CEOs who would use a calendar for the time of day can deny the need to speak out for their company's—and their own —positions on a score of urgencies. Evidence that this demand is recognized and beginning to be acceded to, is seen in a number of recent and peculiar press conferences, as well as in a variety of "President's messages" appearing in print advertising or thinly disguised as socially conscious television commercials. Ditto the occasional gambit of urging the public to pick up its telephone and call the president of the company, collect, in order to rectify dealer apathy to complaints.

It is odd, then, that with the need, the logic, and the success attending the chief executive as communicator-in-chief, the average individual, even with an IQ of 120, can name only three or four CEOs who are outspoken, articulate, and credible. When one is asked to name a round dozen of such enlightened corporate chiefs, out of the thousands of public companies, a certain amount of stammering takes place. By the same token, it's hardly surprising that the few presidents or chairmen who are real communicators are also those same persons who enjoy a special niche in their industries and their communities. They are also those who do more than mouth inanities about the societal obligations which today are intrinsic to industry.

The obvious example of the CEO in the act of communicat-

ing is in speeches to a particular public. The mechanical ver-
balizing of a batch of large-typed pages is not what is meant.
Rather, it is in the preparation of such speeches or talks that one
finds the indicators of a chief executive's calibre as a communicator. Does the CEO just summon the corporate public relations director and say: "Whip up something for me to give at
the regional meeting in Washington on Thursday night"? Or,
does the CEO remain sequestered, with instructions not to be
disturbed, three sharp pencils and a legal-sized, lined, yellow
pad? Or, is it somewhere between these extremes?

Results of the survey of the nation's top 1000 companies
revealed that just over one-third of the CEOs write their own
speeches—or even a draft of them. Some 35 percent of the corporate chiefs felt obligated, as spokesmen for their organizations, to do their own writing. However, respondents to the
questionnaire admitted that 37 percent of the chief executives
instructed their public relations directors as to what to write,
left the actual writing to them, but did make changes in the
resulting manuscripts. Almost a quarter—24 percent—played it
safe and asked for drafts of possible speech material from a
number of executives. Generally, such actions produce what
some perceptive journalists refer to as "spayed speeches." The
remaining 10 percent apparently never give speeches or talks.
Or if they do, they rely on the "speech fairy" to deposit the
scripts under their desk blotters, secretly, during the night.

On a less structured basis, in an area in which communication is more "off-the-cuff," another question was posed to determine the chief executive's ability as an impromptu communicator. Again, the results showed modesty and self-
effacement on the part of the presidents and chairmen. In only
three cases did the CEOs feel any urgency about assuming the
role of corporate spokesman.

Talking to a congressman on public issues topped the list of
one-on-one relationships that the chief executives handled in
person, according to 47 percent of the respondents. Next in importance for the president to take care of personally, some 40
percent said, was answering a reporter or writer, of either a national or local publication, but the journalist had to be important

and seeking information about a company's stand on a public issue. This is surprising, since it is slightly higher than the 38 percent who believed that the CEO would personally want to field a security analyst's questions about the company's financial posture.

Although these three areas had the highest percentages of personal involvement by the chief executive, they were only about one-quarter of the total. Way down in the scorings were three other areas in which the chief executive might respond in person: (1) giving an official of an environmental protection agency the corporate view on air and water pollution standards, with 15 percent; and tieing with 13 percent each were (2) talking to a union official about up-coming negotiations, and (3) responding to a spokesperson for a consumer group seeking an explanation for undesirable company practices. All other fields of confrontation, which might involve any of a dozen other publics, are apparently left to subordinate executives to defend the company's policies, procedures, or products.

Using standard categories of communication skills to qualify chief executives, respondents rated presidents and chairmen high in their ability to "receive" information. This is a key ingredient for a successful general administrator. Although communication requires both reception and transmission, the CEOs scored well on only half the qualifications. One could view them as being generally reactive rather than as taking the initiative.

The ratings for the skills were divided into five categories: excellent, high, medium, low, and poor. The "poor" scores were miniscule in number and related to only four of the skills. Significantly, the largest response among the "poor" scores dealt with the ability to speak well or effectively in public.

The ability to hear and absorb both oral and written materials and presentations brought "excellent" scores to 69 percent of the CEOs. But only 29 percent of them were found to be "excellent" in conducting group meetings.

Among other high scores was one showing 59 percent of the corporate chiefs as "excellent" in their appearance as "candid and truthful at press conferences." Only half the presidents or chairmen were considered "excellent" in maintaining order at stockholder meetings.

Just 33 percent of the CEOs were rated as "excellent" in effective public speaking. One feels that perhaps some of the expensive personnel department executive-skills training might well be expended in the executive suite.

Although fewer than 60 percent got an "excellent" score in "appearing candid and truthful at press conferences," astonishingly, only 35 percent were rated "excellent" in appearing sincere and credible in television appearances. Is it possible that the chief executives are still oriented just to print media and have not moved into the age of electronic media? Or, perhaps there's an emanation of integrity that becomes visible in "eyeball" confrontations, but which is missing from electronic impressions.

It is interesting that the survey provided a double check on the chief executive as a poor communicator. For in the answers to a question asking for a list of the pivotal qualities the CEO seeks in subordinate executives, the chief executives scored in the lowest quartile for "articulateness" and "communicativeness."

Although there is an apparent and rapid change in the attitude for the need to "receive and transmit," there's still a substantive communications gap. If the CEO is the only one who has the inputs, the wisdom, and the authority to speak for the corporation, the chief executive has a concomitant obligation to live up to the unprinted title of communicator-in-chief.

The transitional period for chief executives has spawned huge litters of aids for them. One such technique is the use of regular news commentators who are hired to make questioning realistic to CEOs trying to gain experience through role-playing in order to improve their television appearances. For example, *Business Week*, May 4, 1974: "Harry Bridges, Shell Oil Company president, took a two-day course learning to face TV cameras, microphones and aggressive reporters."

The multiplicity of seminars dealing with the top executive's ability to communicate reaches a peak of practicality in the speech schools and speech coaches which thrive on tutoring CEOs in this generally unwanted discipline. According to *Business Week*, which devoted the entire management section of its August 11, 1973, issue to the soaring success of speech schools for executives, major corporations are the biggest customers. Indeed, the list of companies using these schools and coaches reads like a segment of the Fortune 500. *Business Week* points out that chief executives have begun to feel the need to make themselves available to speak against "the wave of controversial anti-establishment speakers who now dominate the college circuits and have lately begun invading the more traditional forums of business." In addition, the article offers, quite seriously, a boxed "feature" of "seven tips for the novice speaker," and these tips are aimed at chief executives.

More and more top executives are beginning to use the "I'm OK—You're OK" communications technique, more formally recognized as transactional analysis, or T.A. to the cognoscenti. Publishing companies view the dozen or so authors of books on T.A. as the hottest properties on the publishing scene today. From *Games People Play* to *Born to Win*, the volumes show transactional analysis as a new language which translates psychological ideas so that nearly anyone can understand and communicate more effectively. All these books are scooped up by executives at a rate which makes their publishers beam and puts the titles on the best-sellers lists. This phenomenon is another pointer to chief executives' desire to become good communicators. It shows that corporate chiefs recognize that without communications, the whole American economic system stands a good chance of corroding.

The credo of the obsolescent chief executive has been: "I provide jobs. I operate profitably. I provide a necessary product or service." Today, new phrases are expected in addition to the old ones, and they add other highly beneficial dimensions. "I speak up, voluntarily and candidly. I speak and commit my company and myself. I respond to the needs of the general public as well as to my industry. I volunteer my beliefs on public issues, unfiltered by a profit motive. I communicate so that society, community, industry, government, and all other pertinent publics will know that I hear, I understand, and I respond."

5
Corporate lying

lie *(lī)* n. 1. A false statement or piece of information deliberately presented as being true; a falsehood. 2. Anything meant to deceive or give a wrong impression.

> *(American Heritage Dictionary of the English Language)*

Use of lies, evasions, half truths, and specious euphemisms by industrial and governmental executives has made these "inethics" part of our morals and codes of behavior. The motivation behind such behavior is: "If it's all right for him, it's okay for me." As in our use of language, if a word or phrase is publicly used for a specific meaning by important figures in education, government, writing, theater, and science—even though it contradicts prior recognized usage—the word or phrase becomes part of our standard language in the new sense.

Thus, the burden of responsibility for integrity rests on the leader—be he the president of the United States, the president of Harvard, or the president of General Motors. That responsibility is concrete and constant.

It is understandable, but not condonable, that the leader cry "national security" or remain silent or act to "protect our stockholders' investments or our employees' welfare." But the threshold between public good and self-interest is extremely low; sometimes, these ambits are scarcely distinguishable. When does "national security" become "personal security"? When does "corporate survival" become "personal survival"?

The emotional triggers are always cocked, and they're easy to pull. All it takes is an evasionary appeal to patriotism or pocketbook.

Lies wear a variety of masks. Behind all of them, though, is the single face of deception. The lies executives tell generally fall into several categories. (Obviously, the list is incomplete, but add your own.)

1. Outright lies
2. Evasions
3. Half-truths
4. True statement followed by false conclusion
5. Silence
6. Literal truth when it's known that the inference will be wrong
7. The nonanswer or nonsequitur
8. The knowing smile while remaining mute
9. Attacking the questioner to avoid answering
10. Answering questions with other questions
11. Ambiguity
12. Postponement
13. Obfuscation or gobbledygook
14. "Salted" paragraphs—a scattering of nuggets of truth in a quantity of false dross

Consider, for instance, the case of the vice-president of an industrial-equipment manufacturing firm whose infantile evasions of the facts of his education earned him contempt and mockery. For some reason, he wanted people to believe that he was a graduate of Harvard rather than of the small midwestern state university he actually attended. He wore a Harvard crimson tie at all times and referred as frequently as possible to such sayings as, "In Cambridge it's thus and so . . ." If someone at a meeting asked: "Well, what's the proper Harvard response to this or that?" he'd respond, "Is a Harvard man supposed to have a different reaction?" Or, when asked if he'd gone to a recent class reunion, he'd laugh and say, "No. My class was 1930." It was, but at State U.

Childish? Of course. But it's an example of the ethics of a business leader and mass employer. It was an indicator of the man's immorality. Later, he was caught squirreling away company funds; it was his lying which opened up the case. Like the proverbial iceberg, lies are only the visible tip of a mass of immorality.

Security analysts and researchers for financial firms exist primarily because of the accepted recognition that in a majority of cases, presidents and chairmen of publicly held companies do not hesitate to sign the deliberately misleading double-talk known as the president's letter or the chairman's letter on page one of most annual and interim reports. The analysts and researchers are hired, and work hard, to get behind the chief executive's words; to get the bald and often painful facts for their employers' customers, who are getting more and more skeptical. Too often in the past, stockholders and prospective investors believed those "cautiously optimistic" statements, only to wind up wiping the egg off their faces with the crying towel of: "But the annual report said . . ." It's no wonder that analysts and researchers tear the tables and charts out of the annual reports, deep-sixing all those positive phrases in the front of the book.

Just take the first ten 1973 annual reports you can get your hands on and compare what was said with what actually happened. Of course, you won't find outright lies, but you will discover some of the ways used to keep you from selling your stock or to persuade you to make an investment in the company. And you'll find, also, that although the statements are *literally* true, more often than not they are deliberately written to give a different impression from what the chief executive knows to be reality.

This popular but pernicious form of lying could be eliminated quite simply if chief executives told their report writers: "Just put down the facts in such a manner that the readers' inferences will be correct. Let's say what we know or sincerely believe, not what we want the stockholders to believe." According to Wall Street writers, that attitude would be beneficial rather than detrimental. A real credibility would be built up, and the company's stock price would stabilize. Consequently, the P/E ratio would more nearly reflect the company's actual posture.

Chief executives have long victimized their own public relations directors by making them party to a given activity or policy without giving them a voice in the decision-making process. They're asked to become the spokesmen for policies which are *faits accomplis*. Once this happens, PR directors become principal actors on stage and lose their effectiveness as counsellors and advisors in their own discipline. Under such circumstances, some PR persons become totally embittered. They usually quit and search for the shining urn of client perfection. Still others stay and bleed. They become latter-day Elishas. However, some stay and win in their efforts to bring their chiefs to realistic evaluation of their policies.

Since it's not our purpose to invite litigation for libel, the names of persons or companies (except those that have been highly publicized) will not be used in the sampling that follows. Generally, though, upper-management readers will probably recognize the participating players. For example, Watergate, its personnel, and activities, are still fresh and odorous. The multitude of lies, uttered or implied, are right out in front for all to see. It's a gemstone example of the autohypnosis concomitant with "We're doing this for their good."

But how about the corporation (one of Fortune's 1000) which changed its auditing firm—one of the most prestigious in the country—because the accountants refused to use a system which they believed portrayed the company in an "inexact financial posture" and would make an upcoming quarter look highly profitable? This effort at short-run profitability is hardly the area for ethics or truth.

There's a large electronics firm which recently laid off some 10,000 employees out of a work force of 45,000. The situation was unfortunate for those laid off, but is necessary on occasion, as any manager can understand. However, a different scene is revealed when it suddenly becomes apparent that the majority of those let go had been with the company for between

10 and 20 years, had seniority, and were in the $15,000–$20,000 salary bracket. Now, at the same time, this company was hiring new graduates, at about $650 per month. Could anyone imagine that the laid-off employees believed that management was telling the truth in the reasons given for their termination?

It's anyone's guess as to the number of companies fighting (overtly or otherwise) so that it will not become mandatory to have the same language in the annual reports as that supplied, hopefully in confidence, to the Securities and Exchange Commission. The reason usually vouchsafed is that in the 10–K forms there is too much confusing detail for the stockholders. The language in the annual report must be simpler, more understandable, more palatable—and perhaps quite revealing. No one could really call that lying—or could he?

No newspaper or magazine reader, no radio listener, no TV watcher needs to be handed examples of fraudulent product claims, false statements, misleading implications, phony artwork, or faked-up photography in the hundreds of advertising messages that come forth daily. These cannot be labeled anything but management-approved lies. There is no justification in *caveat emptor*.

Consideration must also be given to the corporate ethics in the buying and selling of securities as a result of information released or withheld. Two of the more flamboyant examples —McDonnell Douglas and Gulf & Western—have been minutely detailed in the nation's financial and business press. The SEC has a staff of lawyers fighting for "timely and proper disclosure"—for that, read "truth." And every word is vital.

The practice of making press releases about predictions of profitable quarters and full-year earnings is declining now. Untold thousands of persons have lost heavily because of their reliance on what "the president of the company promised." (Remember the Four Seasons (AMEX) case?) The prediction syndrome is undergoing "prudent man" treatment. In some cases, management has learned that eating one's forecasts leaves an unhappy aftertaste. In other cases, PR executives have been able to demonstrate that it's good business practice and makes for credibility to stay away from the optimistic futures, which sometimes reflect a cover-up for known negative or mediocre next quarters.

Many examples of total silence when up-coming news will be bad are available to any reader of financial publications. Plant closings and attendant firings do not happen overnight or unexpectedly. Corporation chiefs insist that their PR departments remain mute, despite the fact that they know that eventually they will have to answer the question "Why didn't you tell us when you made the decision, so that we could have taken some steps to protect our community?" Media people refer to these as "submarine lies."

Unhappily, most corporate chief executives do not realize that outsiders view the press release (even when attribution is to some lesser executive) as the direct word from the mountain top. On the obverse, when the glaring light of exposure of wrong or omission of positive statements or actions occurs, corporate chiefs are of the opinion that their various publics will blame some subordinate and that the president will even get a sympathetic nod for being the victim of staff malfeasance. They couldn't be more in error. The press—and through them the public as well as the company's own employees—know that the president's integrity is never subverted by subordinates. The president, whose moral standards overlie the entire company, in effect dictates the organization's ethics and the resulting impression the public has of it. The corporate chief can't say, "I didn't know anything at all about it" and expect that to be swallowed. Nor can the CEO crawl under the blanket of "Everyone says (or does) things like that." For it is the president, and the president alone, who stands naked under the stone-faced stare of increasingly sophisticated and skeptical publics. The corporate chief can't expect respect or philosophical acceptance from peers by jettisoning those executives at whose door the baby is found.

The chief executive's own code is the one under which the company operates. Any subordinate who doesn't fit that criterion stands a pretty good chance of being fired—or rather, of never having been hired.

A significant majority of the public relations practitioners in this country are of the solid opinion that theirs is the responsibility for the "conscience of the corporation." It's the PR executive who is accountable for the words and language of the company's announcements and responses and who must remonstrate with the chief: "No. We can't do this or say that." The PR director must not only recommend philosophy, policy, and activity based on an urgent sense of accuracy and integrity, but also see that it is achieved. Otherwise, the PR executive must leave the company, for the PR posture of the organization rests with this person.

There's a saying among public relations people: "No job's worth anything unless you're willing to put your head on the block for it." However, the burden must eventually return to its source, the chief executive. He is the Procrustes to the PR director's prisoner. Unless the PR executive conforms to the chief's standards, someone will be found who does. It was tougher in the days of the legendary Greek giant Procrustes, who grabbed passers-by and fit them to his iron bed. If they were too short, they were stretched. If they were too tall, they were lopped down to size.

However, there is no absolute. There are times and circumstances when an executive can look at four ounces of liquid in an eight-ounce glass, and say, "It's half full," without being wrong or lying, or unethical. This is called "situational ethics," but it is valid only when an adversary condition exists. However, in a situation in which questions cannot be asked, the chief executive has no option as to whether the glass is "half full" or "half empty." At such times the CEO must say, "There are four ounces of an unknown liquid in an eight-ounce glass." The chief would be on safe ground to continue and say, "Some might say that it's half empty, but I choose to call it half full, for the following reasons . . ."

"White lies" and the circumstances that call them into being are condonable—and sometimes commendable as is apparent—for a man who has demonstrated integrity in the past. It's situational ethics again. And there are times when any response to questioning is both impractical and unethical— when the jobs of thousands could be jeopardized, when negotiations

between companies could be endangered and which, if successful, could benefit everyone. For instance, the directors of Company A have decided it would be beneficial to acquire finan-
cially weak Company B. If acquired, Company B's employees
would be assured of continuing employment. Both A's and B's
stockholders would benefit by the synergism of the merger and
resultant increased earnings. B's plant communities would continue their tax advantages if the plants didn't have to close for
lack of operating capital. Even A's customers would benefit
from broader product selection, etc., etc. However, if word
about the decision to go into negotiations should leak out pre-
maturely, arbitrageurs would move in, the price of B's stock
would shoot up, and A wouldn't be able to swing the deal.

Now, onto the scene comes a financial writer who has
somehow sniffed out the possible merger. He calls Company A
and asks, "I hear that you're planning to take over Company B.
Anything to it?" What answer can be given that will be truthful
and yet not endanger the negotiations? Obviously, A cannot say,
"Yes. It's correct." Equally obviously, A cannot say, "No. Nothing to it." And "no comment" is as good as saying "yes" in
this case. Refusing to talk to the reporter will only result (if he's
normally aggressive) in a news item reading: "Reports on the
Street have it that Company A will take over Company B. Officials at neither company could be reached for comment."

Although the problem seems insoluble, one major
corporation's PR director and his chief executive worked out a
method for handling such situations, at a time when the company was on an acquisition spree. He called a press conference for financial writers and other pertinent press people. He
cited a set of circumstances similar to this and posed his problem to those present. After two heavy hours of discussion, he
got agreement on a mode of procedure. He promised that any
other reporters who called would get the same response that
he'd give those present who called in the future: "We won't say
'no.' We won't say 'yes.' We won't say 'no comment.' We're always looking at possibilities. When we have definite news of
negotiation activity which we can release without jeopardizing
the deal, we'll provide all the data to all of you at the same
time." And it worked for years.

The operative word in each case is "intent." And intent is a mirror image of integrity. Today, in a world in which corporate guilt is presumed, there is a need for initiative, if not aggressive integrity. Our civilization has so disillusioned us by its assumption that lies are acceptable if the short-term need is to be served, that we've become much like some European countries (not necessarily behind the Iron Curtain) in which one must prove his innocence, rather than the reverse.

Integrity and morality are old-fashioned words, but they're the qualities that we desperately search for in our relations with one another. Those who lead us must be those who display these qualities. It is not enough to claim partial allegiance to ethics, for integrity is like pregnancy. One can't have just a little bit of it.

Corporate leadership which, because it is exposed and emulated, must settle for no less than total integrity. For corporate executives ape the moral attitudes of those who govern us. If a country's leader accepts, condones, or connives at corruption—or even seems to do so—then we can expect similar policies from the senior managements of the nation's top companies. And then, in almost immediate resonance, the public ethos vibrates to the same pitch.

The morass of sordidness detailed to an almost unbelieving public during the history-making telecasts of the House Judiciary Committee hearings, which resulted in the decision to impeach the President of the United States, was enough to make even the most cynical viewer, politician or layman, retch in revulsion.

Now the chief executives of our major companies must break out of the example-following rhythm to eliminate the syndrome of "If it's okay for them, it's okay for us." Chief executives must create their own wave of rising expectations, increase it to demands, and insist on nothing less than total openness and honesty.

What stronger signal do they need than the traumatic resignation of the President of the United States in a soul-rattling admission of obstruction of justice and a mass of amoral maneuverings; a Vice-President, resigned under threat of prosecution for corruption; a federal judge convicted of shocking wrongdoing; a senator desperately defending himself under charges of selling influence; a Treasury Secretary indicted for bribery and perjury (and

concomitant with it an industry representative confessing to brib-
ing that cabinet officer); a lieutenant governor convicted of lying
to a senate committee; and a score of the nation's chief executives'
hand-picked aides and counsellors indicted or convicted for vil-
lainies that none would willingly tolerate in his own home or
business?

In the past, the organizations which speak for industry as a
whole (Chamber of Commerce, National Association of Manufacturers, etc.) have been loudly articulate against hints of violation
of the "American system of free enterprise and what it stands for."
But there's been an uncanny silence at the destruction of the
American code of ethics during this menopause of morality the
nation has been suffering.

The famous worm is squirming and seems to be turning. The
public—consumer and employee—is demanding a return and an
adherence to the cardinal tenets of simple honesty and an ethical
standard of morality. The chief executives of our top companies
should be listening.

Nearly every PR practitioner, corporate executive or outside consultant, is optimistic about new values in the future.
They are agreed that the PR executive is being brought more
often into the early phases of policy construction. They feel that
this will help them in keeping their companies' statements and
actions at a higher level, thus avoiding all but the most cavilling
of recriminations. They sincerely believe that top management
generally is more open, more aware of ethical appearances, and
is setting a more rigid scale of moral values for themselves,
their peers, and their subordinates.

III
HARD-CORE
ACCOUNTABILITY

6
$E^2 + C^2 = P +$

The age of hard-core accountability is now. No longer are chief executives judged solely by their ability to maximize profits and stay within the rules of the game. Today, they are judged by their corporation's total impact on people, society, and the physical environment. The public looks beyond bare profits to the socially redeeming qualities accompanying them, just as the Supreme Court justices in their recent ruling on hard-core pornography looked beyond the appeal to prurient interests to the presence of elements of serious literary, artistic, political, or scientific values. Without the plus of social values, profits, like pornography, are condemned. The ROI is no longer absolute monarch of industry.

To qualify for public acceptance, the chief executive must consider more factors than ever before. For example, it isn't enough to make and sell a product profitably. The chief executive must also consider the scarce resources that go into it, the pollution caused by making and consuming it, the satisfaction it provides the consumer, and the possible undesirable consequences of its consumption.

When scientists needed a cosmic equation to help them understand the new atomic age, Einstein provided them with his famous $E = mc^2$. On a different level, we offer $E^2 + C^2 = P +$, which is not intended as a mathematically valid equation, but rather as a symbol to stimulate the chief executive to look beyond the usual variables of revenues, costs, and profits to the broader ones required in this age of hard-core accountability.

Each of the following chapters in Part III deals with one of the four variables on the left-hand side of the equation and its relationship to a profits-plus criterion of accountability. Our E^2 covers environmental exigencies, discussed in Chapter 7, and "evil" employees, discussed in Chapter 8. Our C^2 covers consumerism (Chapter 9) and conservation of energy and materials (Chapter 10). These four factors cover only part of the spectrum of full accountability. But they illustrate that the scope of business responsibility can no longer be confined by the artificial and defensive boundaries drawn by lawyers and economists. The first lesson of hard-core accountability is that the social impact of a company's regular business activities cannot be escaped. The second lesson is that the stubborn reckoning of Nature can no longer be ignored. Mother Nature has beaten the women's lib movement to a seat on the board of directors.

The main purpose of this chapter is to serve as a preface to a full consideration of these lessons of hard-core accountability. First, we examine how committed the chief executive is to the doctrine of social responsibility by reviewing Question 5 of our survey. Then, we analyze the CEO's ranking of 12 social problems and the underlying social attitudes and values that are reflected.

Our survey projects the image of a chief executive who has burrowed too long on the bottom line of profits. Like the tunnel worker who must be brought up to the earth's atmosphere, the chief executive needs to be placed in a decompression chamber in order to avoid the pain of the transition. Hopefully, exposure to new social and ecological values ease the chief executive's passage.

Question 5 asked what degree of responsibility the chief executive was willing to accept beyond that of making a profit for stockholders. Responses to five areas of social responsibility are summarized in the table on p. 65.

The large number of total responses in the "partly" column —653, which constitutes 55 percent of the grand total—charac-

	Completely No. (%)	Partly No. (%)	Not at all No. (%)	N.A. or Other No. (%)
a) To make financial contributions to educational and charitable institutions	94 (39)	119 (50)	16 (6)	9 (4)
b) To provide salaried personnel for philanthropic work	38 (16)	127 (53)	58 (24)	15 (6)
c) To help solve social problems	49 (21)	148 (62)	30 (13)	11 (5)
d) To devote time to civic activities	59 (25)	134 (56)	38 (16)	7 (3)
e) To initiate action in response to community needs	56 (24)	125 (53)	43 (18)	14 (6)
Total responses:	296 (25)	653 (55)	185 (16)	56 (5)
Grand total:	1190			

terizes the basic attitude of the chief executive toward social responsibility, i.e., muddle-headed and ambivalent. However, it is encouraging to find that 25 percent of the total responses are in the "completely" column, compared to 16 percent in the "not at all" column. The leaning of chief executives as a whole appears to be in the direction of accepting social responsibility. Strengthening this impression is the fact that the 25 percent totally in favor of the listed social responsibility actions, added to the 55 percent partly in favor, add up to 80 percent, as compared to 15 percent who oppose these actions.

Of those in opposition, a review of the individual questionnaires shows that only six chief executives—2.5 percent—reject all five areas of social responsibility. This finding proves that only slight support exists for Milton Friedman's extreme view that business should do what it is chartered to do and can do best, namely, to make profits. However, his view is in direct contrast to the ideology expressed in an increasing number of corporate annual reports. An excellent example appeared in the 1970 annual report of BankAmerica Corporation: "Any company, and certainly any bank, must include in its own balance sheet some recognition of the state of health of the community it serves. The corporation, by virtue of its own enlightened self-interest, the consciences of its officers, and the expectations of the public, has a role to play in the process of solving contemporary ills."

Despite the affirmativeness of this statement, it should be noted that the primacy of profits is not challenged. In fact, the statement continues by saying that "in the long pull, nobody can expect to make profits—or have any meaningful use for profits—if our entire society is wracked by tensions."

Of the five areas of social responsibility covered in our survey, endorsement of financial contributions to educational and charitable institutions is highest, winning complete approval of 39 percent. Considering the historical precedent established by such philanthropists as Andrew Carnegie and John D. Rockefeller, this is not surprising. Public policy has institutionalized such giving through the IRS rule that allows a tax deduction of up to five percent of pretax profits. Furthermore, the courts have upheld public and legislative acceptance of corporate philanthropic activity, as evidenced in such cases as *A. P. Smith Manufacturing Co.* v. *Barlow.*

The actual percentage of pretax profits given averaged 1.12 percent for the seven-year period 1965–1971. A few corporations give more. For example, Levi Strauss & Co. enjoys a golden reputation for routinely allocating three percent of its net profits to community projects.

In light of the almost universal acceptance of corporate philanthropy, it was surprising to find 16 chief executives in our sample of the nation's 1000 largest firms who totally reject this form of social responsibility. This attitude points to these men as myopic corporate Scrooges whose time period could be that of the diplodocus. As if confirming this image, the questionnaire of one of them, who also rejected all four other areas of responsibility, described him as possessing all but one negative personality trait.

But there is another plausible explanation—the belief that "buying your way out" of social responsibility simply isn't a relevant response to today's problems. This explanation is supported by two observations about the chief executives who don't favor corporate financial contributions: three chief executives do accept obligations in all of the four other areas; two believe that salaried personnel should be provided or that the chief executive should devote some time to civic activities. In other words, a more specific exercise of social responsibility was demanded.

Studies other than our survey also show that business preoccupation with philanthropy as the sole or major expression of social responsibility is declining. For example, a study by Meinolf Dierkes, Rob Coppock, and others concerning areas of social concern mentioned in the annual reports of a sample of Fortune 500 companies reports that reference to "philanthropic and social involvement" declined from 80 percent in 1967 to 22 percent in 1971. During the same period, mention of "environmental" topics rose from 10 percent to 42 percent, and consumer protection rose from 7 percent to 11 percent.

Dan Fenn's study, "Executives as Community Volunteers," shows disenchantment by younger executives with low risk, conventional community involvement in traditional community social organizations. What they seek is more meaningful participation with contemporary organizations that address themselves to the solution of social problems. They also want to be involved in policy formulation, not just implementation.

In response to employee demands for greater social involvement, Xerox, IBM, and a few other companies have provided paid leaves of absence for the purpose. Xerox's Social Service Leave program, launched in the fall of 1971, is the best known. Xerox employees in the United States who have been with the company three years or more can take up to a year's absence with full pay and benefits to work with social service organizations of their choosing. In 1971, 20 employees were granted one-year leaves. Their projects have aided alcoholics, migrant children, the retarded, minorities and youth, drug addicts, prisoners, the elderly, and the afflicted. Among their activities have been the teaching of practical photography, tutoring and counselling minority college and pre-college students, and helping ex-prisoners and prospective parolees find employment.

Despite this outstanding example, our survey shows that this kind of corporate responsibility gets the lowest acceptance among the five areas covered. Only 16 percent of the chief executives accepted the responsibility of lending salaried personnel "completely"; 53 percent, "partly"; and 24 percent, "not at all." The attitude toward devoting personal time to civic activities is slightly better: the percentage of "partly" responses is about the same (56 percent), but more chief executives approve of this activity "completely"—25 percent.

More than any other area of social responsibility, the providing of salaried personnel most visibly interferes with the regular business of making a profit. This reason, we believe, accounts for the fact that chief executives accept it the least.

Two other areas also involve a major diversion of attention from the primary goal of making a profit—helping to solve social problems and initiating action in response to community needs. These are third and fourth in order of acceptance as measured by responses completely or partly in favor of these actions.

Although chief executives can justify such social expenditures in the name of making long-run profits, their hesitancy to do so can be explained by arguments other than Friedmanesque interference with the corporation's economic function. Voluntary expenditures—and that's the essence of social responsibility—may place the corporation at a competitive disadvantage if other corporations don't do likewise. For example, if one lumber company spends millions on pollution abatement but others don't, its higher production costs will make it unattractive to investors and customers.

Other reasons for shunning social problem-solving are more philosophical. There's no special reason why chief executives should know what's good for society, and because they have no special qualifications in the social area, they tend to be flocculent. It has also been argued that the extension of corporate activity into social areas amounts to a form of totalitarianism.

Nonetheless, there is increasing evidence in annual reports and special studies that corporations are responding to the social crises of cities and the nation. The list of projects is impressive: recruiting, training, and hiring disadvantaged employees; supporting black capitalism; installing pollution abatement equipment; drug education; housing construction and rehabilitation; community planning; and support of education. A special study by the Human Resources Network, *Profiles of Involvement,* catalogues 535 social-action projects of 186 of the nation's largest corporations.

How far chief executives are willing to move in the direction of greater social involvement depends in large measure on how threatening the external environment becomes and whether government and other institutions are able to cope with social problems. For this reason, Question 6 asks company presidents to assign a priority to a list of 12 social problems. The ranking of each, ranging from a very low of one to a very high of five, is listed in Fig. 1. A comparison of the two top-priority concerns with the three lowest ones shows that chief executives are oriented to problems that affect short-run profits and immediate survival, despite their knowledge that corporate welfare is based only on long-term profitability.

The energy crisis and inflation became the main acute problems in 1973 and continue to be. These are the chief executives' first- and second-priority problems, respectively. Their impact on profits is immediate and direct, even though they also have long-run implications.

In contrast, the bottom-ranking social problems can be put on the back burner. Political reform at local, state, and national levels, stabilization of the social order, and preserving natural resources are weighty, complex problems that chief executives like to talk about in their speeches, but which they never quite find time to get around to. The CEO may even ask a vice-president for public affairs to give some thought to them, but then neglects to ask what progress is being made. Yet when a crisis occurs, such as the urban crisis of 1967, the CEO complains bitterly that subordinates have failed, that the early warning system didn't work. Now, the problem is on the "speed" burner, and the CEO has to make time available not to work out

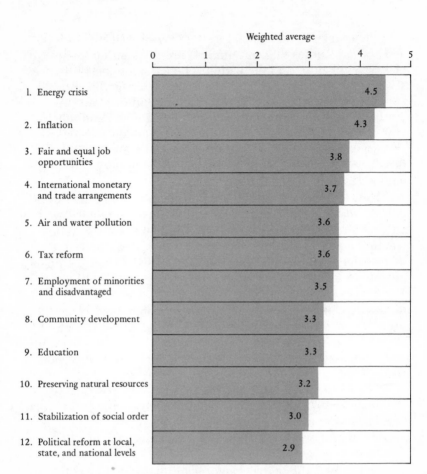

FIG. 1. Priorities assigned to 12 social problems.

basic solutions, but just enough to get past another hot summer until the next profit-and-loss statement is due.

These crises have served a useful purpose, for they point out the strengths and weaknesses of the chief executive's ability to solve social problems. On the one hand, we see an enormously resourceful person who is willing to meet with peers from other corporations, cooperate with government, and even sit down with adversaries from the social sector. One of the best examples is Henry Ford, II, who on the national level, at the suggestion of President Johnson, organized the National Alliance of Businessmen. On the local level, he headed the blue-ribbon New Detroit Committee. Both groups sought to quell social unrest by providing more jobs for minorities. Henry Ford was admirably suited for these tasks, for he was described by *Fortune* as "by any standard a more contemporary man than ever—broader in outlook and understanding, involved in a greater range of activities, and more closely attuned to the social and political realities of his country and the world."

The New Detroit Committee seemed to have an excellent chance of success because of its leadership and the composition of its membership. It included national black leaders, young ghetto militants, and Detroit's top business leadership. But now, we see the weakness of business leadership in the social arena, for the Committee failed. It did not create confidence among the black population in the Detroit area, nor did it help give them hope for the future. The main reason for this failure has been attributed to the inability of these business leaders to establish a dialogue with the local poverty organizations. As stated by the *Wall Street Journal:* "But instead of forming a dialogue, the committee is finding itself stalled over communications—the very gap it was supposed to close. Some of its have-not spokesmen have already quit the panel, intensifying the problem."

However, when a way is found to increase the private benefits from social investments, they receive quicker high-level attention. One of the best examples is the famous Boston Urban Redevelopment Program (BURP) innovated by Eli Goldston, the late chairman of Eastern Gas & Fuel. By requiring the installation of gas furnaces and kitchen stoves in houses renovated by a company-backed group for occupancy by low-income families, his investment of manpower and resources paid off.

The absence of pressure from the government or a social-action group also explains a low ranking. This is why "employment of minorities and disadvantages" is ranked seventh, whereas "fair and equal job opportunities," associated with legally enforced programs, is ranked far up, in third place. Chief executives are all too aware of the existence of the Equal Employment Opportunity Commission (EEOC), the requirement that EEO–1 reports be submitted and the omnipresence of the women's lib movement and such organizations as the National Organization for Women (NOW).

Pressure to respond and the relationship to short-run profits explain the ranking of the remaining three issues. International monetary and trade arrangements, air and water pollution, and tax reform are not yet at a crisis stage, but they do have an economic impact that affects profits. International monetary and trade arrangements, like inflation, affect the price parameter within which a company must operate; air and water pollution abatements costs affect a company's competitive position; and tax reform determines after-tax profits.

In summary, the chief executive gives highest priority to short-term profits and responds to broad social and political problems only when a crisis occurs. It's the money game that interests him. A large pile of green counters at the end of each year's game ensures applause by stockholders, the financial community, and fellow chief executives.

As long as the social game is a voluntary, peripheral activity, it will not occupy much of the chief executive's time. But as we have stressed and shown throughout this book, the age of confrontation has pushed the social game into the executive suite.

Hard-core accountability means that the two games must now be played simultaneously and that one has an effect on the other. Not only green counters, but also the golden goodwill ones must be collected to remain in business.

C.H.W. 7.74

7
Environmental exigencies

Environmental exigencies have extended the range of the chief executive's responsibilities. To the normal economic goal of staying in the black must be added the physical goal of keeping the skies and waters blue and the human goal of enhancing the quality of life.

Organizational boundaries that delimit the corporation's scope of responsibility are stretched far beyond the walls of the corporation. They include any geographical region and group of people affected by the company's operations or use of its products. Air currents and waterways carry the pollutants and effluents of factories to the surrounding neighborhood, nearby communities and states, and even other countries. The public places responsibility for the harm caused to land, wildlife, buildings, and people on the corporate heads of those organizations to whom the pollutants can be traced.

The implications of environmental considerations are obviously so complex and far-reaching that the temptation for company presidents and chairmen to try to put things off as long as possible is exceedingly great. Their option to do so, however, varies with the nature of the environmental problem. There are three types of problems: (1) those that require an immediate response because of their emergency nature; (2) those of an ongoing polluting nature, for which the temptation to postpone action is offset by increasing political pressures and legal requirements; and (3) those affecting the ecosystem which can be postponed indefinitely, except when unusual ecological stresses occur.

The first of these types of problems has historical significance in that environmental burdens were first thrust upon chief executives in the form of emergencies. The most dramatic of these were the break-up of the giant oil tanker *Torrey Canyon*, the "blowout" of Union Oil Company's well six miles off the shore of Santa Barbara, and the collision of two Standard Oil of California tankers in San Francisco harbor. All of these disasters required quick clean-up efforts by the companies involved.

Other environmental events also disturbed the public. Prolonged smog caused sickness and deaths as early as 1948 in Donora, Pennsylvania, and, later, in such metropolises as Los Angeles, New York, and Cleveland. To combat the danger of smog, public officials were given the power to temporarily shut down industry and restrict motor vehicle usage.

In these emergency situations, company heads responded quickly and decisively or cooperated with public officials. These events had the advantage of being short-lived and therefore minimally disruptive of company operations. But because of their newsworthy nature, each emergency placed the corporate image in mortal danger. Extraordinary care was taken by some companies, such as Standard Oil of California, to demonstrate to the news media that they took their environmental responsibilities seriously. Also, these companies prepared contingency plans to handle future eventualities.

Although the environmental emergencies attracted the most attention, it is the second type of environmental problem—ongoing pollution—that continues to plague chief executives the most. Our survey reflects this concern: 24 percent of the company presidents and chairmen assign air and water pollution a "very high" priority; another 32 percent assign a "high" priority. Only the energy crisis—which is certainly related to the environment—inflation, fair and equal job opportunities, and international monetary and trade arrangements get higher priority.

But although they give attention to environmental problems, corporate chiefs would rather not meet personally with outsiders on this subject. Only 15 percent of our chief executives would personally handle an inquiry from an official of an environmental protection agency seeking company views on air and water pollution standards. A likely explanation for this ambivalence is that basically, chief executives are still fighting the notion of bearing the financial burden of social costs. These are the side effects of production—items that are not considered in corporate accounting systems. As the economist Kenneth Boulding once said of our economic system, "We make people pay for the *goods* they produce, but do not make them pay for the *bads*."

In the past, social costs, or externalities, could be ignored; nature's ability to renew itself was not overtaxed, and few people were affected. Now, however, social costs have become an economic and political issue because of population growth and rapid industrialization. The pollution of streams, rivers, and oceans and the loss of forest lands and wildlife are bemoaned not only by a handful of conservationists, but by multitudes of leisure-seekers who enjoy the outdoors and are willing to organize to protect their newfound rights. Nature has attracted spokesmen who must now be accorded the same consideration as other business constituencies. As the economist would remind us, in the trilogy of factors of production—land, labor, and capital—land seems to be reasserting its status after decades of neglect.

Confronting the chief executive is a well-organized environmental movement backed up with comprehensive and stringent legislation and judicial support. Traditional conservation groups, such as the Sierra Club, the Izaak Walton League, the National Wildlife Federation, and the Wilderness Society, have been joined by new environmentalists who believe in strong and immediate action. Partly because of this challenge to their status, even the older groups have become more activist. The Sierra Club and Friends of the Earth, for example, have devoted much of their resources to legal action. Some newer groups, such as the Environmental Defense Fund and the National Resources Defense Council, rely exclusively on this tactic and often choose well-known adversaries, such as Walt Disney Enterprises (in the Mineral King case) and Secretary of the Interior Rogers Morton (in the Alaska Pipeline case), in order to receive wide publicity.

Largely as a result of the success of these environmental groups, pollution-abatement requirements are now formalized in legislation. Whatever discretion the chief executive had to control pollution voluntarily or to obey lackadaisically enforced laws is now gone. Even the Old Refuse Act of 1899, which was blatantly ignored by companies and unenforced by the Corps of Engineers, is now heeded. New laws, such as the 1967 Air Quality Act, the 1970 Clean Air Act Amendments, and the Federal Water Pollution Control Act of 1972, are far-reaching and stringent. These laws establish strict standards and deadlines within which business must operate. For example, the auto industry has been sharply aware that emissions of carbon monoxide and hydrocarbons must be reduced by at least 90 percent of 1970 levels for 1975 models and emissions of nitrogen oxides by 90 percent for 1976 models.

The chief executive's response to legislation and pressures from environmental groups has been ambivalent and reluctant. On the one hand, the CEO realizes that business will have to bear part of the estimated $274 billion that the nation can expect to spend on pollution-abatement equipment in the decade from 1972–1981. Furthermore, the chief executive realizes that more than immediate abatement costs are involved. The economic consequences may affect a company's competitive position in the industry, the demand for an industry's products, and corporate profit margins. The CEO is tempted, therefore, to resist legislation. This was clearly seen during the energy crisis, when utilities, oil companies, and other industries sought exemptions from or postponements of regulations. On the other hand, the chief executive is gradually coming to realize that pollution controls are here to stay. Facing up to them will increase the CEO's chances of learning to cope with their far-reaching implications for product design and market development.

The chief executive's leadership role as the company's value-setter extends to redesigning its organizational structure and behavior. According to the Conference Board, many companies have established pollution-control units to deal with abating air and water pollution. But more than this structure is required; the environmental impact of the production process used must also be examined. When CEOs sit down with their engineering staffs to determine the most efficient production process, they must insist that social costs become part of the calculation of production costs. The company's engineers must gradually become imbued with environmental values.

Some chief executives have gone a step further by extending their decision-making process to include environmental groups. One example is the planning of the Henderson molybdenum mining project, which became a landmark of cooperation between the mining industry and environmentalists. Another example is Detroit Edison's cooperative effort with the National Audubon Society to plan a public nature preserve and environmental center on a site 60 miles north of Detroit, where the utility is building two nuclear power plants and an oil-fired plant. Pending is a solution to Reserve Mining Company's egregious habit of dumping tailings into Lake Superior.

In their external political role, chief executives devote much of their attention to environmental public affairs. Their immediate concern is to better refine and define the requirements of existing laws and regulations. They know that companies must now deal with a multitude of federal, state, and local regulatory agencies. One pulp and paper company needed 43 permits from close to a dozen agencies in order to gain approval for its proposed plant expansion. Chief executives also know that interpretations of environmental laws differ widely. For example, the Water Pollution Control Act gives industry until 1977 to install the "best practical" waste-treatment technology and until 1983 to devise "the best available technology economically achievable." When applied to specific industries, these terms obviously invite wide disagreement.

A further question that always arises in chief executives' minds is whether the standards are too stiff and the deadlines too immediate for them to arrive at the most economical solution to pollution-abatement problems. They often appear as spokesmen or witnesses at public hearings in their attempt to modify laws that they consider unreasonable. What upsets chief executives the most is the demand by some environmental extremists to return to or keep the environment at an absolutely pure and natural state. They fear that many people, including public officials, don't understand the need to balance environmental and industrial requirements. Furthermore, they take the viewpoint that pollution is business's problem and that abatement costs can be financed out of profits.

Because of public misconceptions, the chief executive favors public communication on environmental issues, feeling that the lesson of "trade-offs" is particularly important to get across. The public must learn that with each increment of improvement in the environment, there is a cost: higher prices for goods and services, possible declines in employment, restrictions or outright prohibition in the use of some products, and increased taxes. Some of these costs rise sharply as environmental perfection is sought.

While corporate heads try to educate the public, ecologists attempt to educate company presidents and chairmen. Their message is threefold: that business should accept the time frame of eternity, the goal of the ultimate survival of the species, and responsibility for a new constituency of unborn generations. What ecologists seek, in effect, is·to convince chief executives that they must think beyond immediate pollution problems to the third type of environmental problem—the long-term concern for the ecosystem. The ecosystem is the total physical environment on which all life and all activity depend. It deals with how plants and animals relate to one another and to their physical environments. Inherent in this simple definition is the warning that the way in which human beings now live on the earth is tearing its thin, sensitive, life-supporting skin, and ourselves with it, to irreparable tatters. According to Barry Commoner, this is the real environmental crisis. It is not the isolated cases of environmental insult of the first type of environmental problem.

That everything is connected to everything else is the first law of ecology, according to Commoner. An event in one part of the ecosystem has consequences elsewhere as transmitted through its multiple, interconnected parts. These consequences don't usually occur immediately, but accumulate gradually over a period of time. Probably the most publicized example of the workings of the ecosystem is the discovery that DDT sprayed on crops and trees works its way into the food chain of animals and ultimately affects the reproductive power of such animal life as the peregrine falcon, the brown pelican, and the bluebird. DDT became the eco-scare symbol of other unanticipated and disastrous consequences which might befall humans as a result of technological progress. Each dead bird or fish or vanishing species is seen as an indicator of what could happen to us.

Few chief executives are likely to accept these long-range and broad goals. In their capacity as heads of corporations, they can, however, accept a part of this ecological responsibility. Companies must be willing to stop producing or to carefully control the use and disposal of substances that are proved to be harmful to the ecosystem. The restrictions on the sale of DDT are a case in point. However, it is exceedingly difficult to predict which substances will imperil the ecosystem. Ecologists warn that a single substance by itself is seldom the cause of harm; rather, it's the interaction with other elements in nature in a long, causal chain that produces unexpected consequences. For this reason, the best way for chief executives to guard against the possibility that harmful substances will place unusual stress on the ecosystem is to use "closed-loop" production systems wherever possible. One manager of a pulp mill discovered that by producing a number of different products, the wastes of one manufacturing process provided raw materials for another. Process designs thus had more options in their recycling efforts.

Although ecologists have dramatized the relationship of specific substances to the placing of stress on the ecosystem, they are also concerned about the total burden placed on the ecosystem, as measured by the rate of economic growth. They warn that an exponential growth rate simply cannot be sustained. Using the GNP as a measure, a four percent growth rate doubles the GNP every 17 years and quadruples it every 34 years. Thus, ecologists warn business that an ever-rising gross national product should be neither a national goal nor a measure of progress.

The challenge to the GNP has been supported by such studies as *The Limits of Growth*, written by a group of M.I.T. scholars. They conclude that the world's exponential rates of population and industrial growth cannot be sustained for much more than another 100 years. At the same time, some of the country's leading economists have called for new measures of progress. Professors William Nordhaus and James Tobin of Yale propose a "MEW," or "Measure of Economic Welfare," that adds the value of leisure activities to the GNP and subtracts "regrettable expenditures," such as money spent for police protection and for pollution abatement.

These kinds of GNP considerations relate to the much-discussed concept of the quality of life. Many environmentalists believe that self-realization, fulfilling human relationships, love of nature, and aesthetic values should supersede the pursuit of materialistic possessions. Some espouse an ascetic philosophy along the line of Mahatma Gandhi.

By the nature of their position, chief executives are exceedingly skeptical of the no-growth philosophy and brand its proponents as doomsday prophets. Corporate chiefs tend to be optimistic and to place faith in the power of technology—that somehow, our knowledge of nature and ability to control it will enable us to keep the ecosystem in balance. Furthermore, they can point to the need for pollution-abatement equipment as a reason for supporting further growth. Corporate heads see some quality-of-life activities as requiring more, not fewer, products. This is evidenced by the rising leisure-industry market and the increased demand for such things as hiking shoes, backpacks, and snowmobiles.

Despite this justifiable defense of growth in some sectors of the economy, corporate chiefs must be prepared to face slower growth rates in some industries. Utilities and oil companies have already learned that circumstances may justify the replacement of advertising designed to increase sales to advertising urging customers to reduce consumption. Chief executives and their financial constituents—stockholders and security analysts—hope that these periods of scarcity will be short-lived. But ecologists warn us that more such incidents will occur unless population stops rising and people place less of a burden on the environment through an affluent life style.

Since many of these factors are outside the control of chief executives, they are likely to exempt themselves from ecological responsibility for the nation's growth rate or its concept of quality of life. By the same token, they should not be slaves to an ever-rising sales growth curve. Their personal prestige and organizational success should be measured by broader concepts of hard-core accountability that include consideration for environmental impact.

8
"Evil" employees

Edward Gregory, who has worked the 4 p.m.-to-midnight shift for most of his 20-year tenure at GM, committed a company sin. When a United States Senate committee was taking testimony on unsafe cars from Ralph Nader, Gregory called and left a message for Mr. Nader. As later revealed, it concerned a faulty seal in the rear-quarter panels on car bodies that failed to keep out lethal gas. GM subsequently recalled 2,400,000 Chevrolets, at a cost estimate at upwards of $50 million. The recall was effected after several people were found dead in their cars from carbon-monoxide poisoning.

Hero that he was to the consumerists, Gregory would be considered an example of an "evil" employee by most chief executives. It's just another instance of workers not living up to expectations any more—not being committed to the company mission, violating loyalty to management and refusing to work hard.

The younger, better-educated workers particularly gripe the company president. They're the ones who want "higher pay than they deserve" and keep criticizing the president and the system. Some of them really believe this Consciousness III stuff of Charles Reich—that the individual can be liberated, that an ideal society can be constructed in which there are no such things as disciplined "working relationships." These radical ideas seem to be permeating the entire work force—but very slowly.

The chief executive sees further evil in the way personal needs and considerations are put ahead of company requirements. "That's why absenteeism is so high, especially on Fridays and Mondays." Moreover, during good times "workers think nothing of switching jobs, even when the company has invested lots of money training them." Their minds aren't on their work either; "in fact, some of the younger ones are on drugs—or act as if they were."

That they don't seem to have any loyalty or sense of what's right is a further complaint. They seem to find time to join consumerism groups and participate in various social-action causes. A few, like Edward Gregory, even "rat" on the company. And occasionally, you find a group of workers publishing an "underground newspaper and distributing it on company property and time."

No wonder many chief executives find themselves wishing that the clock could be turned back to the good old days when the employer was the undisputed boss. He wouldn't have to put up with all these forms of employee disobedience, because he had complete power to discharge an offending employee.

That power has sharply eroded and along with it, the tables are turned and the employer is accused of being evil. Company presidents are blamed for taking too narrow a view of their obligations, of being overly concerned with economic efficiency and not enough with the welfare of employees and society. He's not living up to the new standards of hard-core accountability.

Chief executives are accused of not really accepting their obligation to provide job safety and satisfaction beyond legal or productivity requirements. Second, they are criticized for allowing a large communication gap to grow between the front office and the shop. Not only do they fail to exert much moral authority over the employees, but the obverse is also true; workers are given little voice in making decisions that affect them. Finally, company presidents are blamed for taking too narrow a view of employees' role as citizens—their right to press for product safety and other socially responsible behavior.

Our survey shows that the chief executive is unlikely to have a background in employee relations and therefore has only limited interest in this area. Only 17 percent of the rankings for the "employee/labor relations" background were in the top three of the eight ranks; only a legal background ranked lower. Our survey also shows that labor-relations matters are not usually seen as causing much of a stir. Answers to Question 7 show that the most typical reaction to a labor ultimatum is the application of standard operating procedures. Only about 30 percent of the chief executives would react by viewing it as a major crisis or showing extreme concern, which is only slightly higher than their reaction to a social-protest group.

No one would quarrel with chief executives' desire to "cool it" in their labor relations or to delegate routine aspects of employee relations. Yet as top boss of a company, the president's attitudes and actions toward people set the human-relations tone for the entire organization. Convinced of the leadership role they must play, some chief executives have enrolled in T-group and other management-training programs. Since 1965 more than 300 chief executives have attended the Presidents' Conferences on Human Behavior, a T-group program set up at the National Training Laboratory. In a report on their experiences, Leland P. Bradford gives the reason for the program's popularity: "More than anyone else perhaps, today's top executives need new and specialized skills in human relations if they are to diagnose and solve the human problems of organizations. The role of the chief executive is becoming increasingly uncertain, complex, and demanding."

Various theories of managerial styles concentrate on one of the three failures of chief executives in the area of employee relations. Douglas McGregor's Theory X vs. Theory Y, Rensis Likert's System Four, and Robert R. Blake and Jane S. Mouton's managerial grid—all point to the need to show greater concern for the motives and attitudes of employees. The managerial grid of Blake and Mouton shows this dimension most clearly. Traditional concern for production is plotted on the horizontal line and the concern for people on the vertical line. Each line has a scale from 0 to 9. In this manner, five types of managerial styles are identified. The old-fashioned boss is a 9,1 type who worries about getting the job done and doesn't give a damn about the workers. The 1,9 type is just the opposite, believing in "country club" management to keep workers happy; production goals are incidental. The 1,1 type isn't good at either task performance or creating job satisfaction, and a 5,5 type tries to balance the two. Obviously, the ideal is the 9,9 boss, who can maximize both concerns.

Showing a concern for employees means different things, depending on whether we're dealing with the supervisory level or top-management level. The chief executive's interest in employees can be shown in two ways—by becoming more visible and by insisting on corporate policies that provide safe and satisfying work conditions.

Politicians know the value of being visible and getting around to their constituents—it shows that they care. Although chief executives don't have to get elected by their employees, they should sometimes act as if they did. Like politicians, chief executives should try to make appearances before every significant segment of their constituency. If possible, they should do what the late Eli Goldston, former chairman of Eastern Gas & Fuel, did. His practice was to visit each plant location at least once a year. And he didn't just talk to the brass or office workers; he went down into the mines, climbed on barges, and went wherever else people worked.

Even if employees only get to see the top boss walking through the shop, a bond forms between them. They get a feeling that the boss is real, and they pay more attention to presidential statements in the company media. Better yet, if the boss stops to talk to a few employees, they will remember the occasion and talk about it with other employees for years to come.

Where the size of the company allows, some enlightened chief executives hold annual employee meetings, perhaps on a regional basis. Here, employees can hear top management's report on the state of the company and prospects for the future. As at stockholder meetings, company officers answer questions from the floor.

Some companies, such as AT&T, Chase Manhattan, Dow Chemical Co., and Smith, Kline & French, cover their annual meetings on closed-circuit television. Chase showed an edited

telecast which dwelt mostly on the slow-paced remarks of the
chairman, David Rockefeller, and the forceful responses of the
bank's president, Williard Butcher, to a stockholder. Company
newscasts typically run continuously throughout the noon hour,
so that most employees can watch it going to or from lunch.

Increasingly, the chief executive and other officers are
learning how to make effective use of the instruments of the
company's internal communication system. The use of television as a warm, face-to-face medium that contributes to team-
building is only one example. But it is doubly significant,
because television reflects the openness and spontaneity of a
modern managerial style. In contrast, exclusive reliance on
print is associated with bureaucracy—stiffness, rigidity, and
control.

Marshall McLuhan notwithstanding, the medium is not the
entire message. What is said and how it is said are what count.
Chief executives who sermonize will reinforce their image as
the top boss, but not as a human one. Chief executives who
insist that every issue of the company newspaper include their
picture will soon be seen as egocentric figureheads. And chief
executives who only talk will not be taken seriously; they must
also act.

The two areas that have in recent years received the most
attention are job safety and job boredom. In 1968 a total of
14,311 people died in industrial accidents, about the same as
the number of American casualties in Vietnam that year.
Another 90,000 suffered permanent impairment. Apparently,
business safety measures had not gone far enough, as the passage of the Occupational Safety and Health Act of 1970 demonstrated. Even now, the National Commission on State Work-
men's Compensation Laws, established by the O.S.H.A.,
concluded that the present state laws are in general neither
adequate nor equitable.

On the matter of job boredom, attention has focused on the
dehumanized conditions of work on the automobile assembly
line. GM's most automated plant—at Lordstown, Ohio, where
Vegas are assembled—illustrates the problem. Despite amen-
ities and high wages for workers, absenteeism and turnover

were staggering and the quality of work abysmally poor. In 1972 the workers rebelled against management, accusing them of a production speedup. Management in turn charged the workers with sabotage. This conflict was highly publicized by the news media and soon became known as the Lordstown Syndrome— a condition of hard and monotonous work whereby workers "feel like nothing."

According to HEW's study *Work in America,* job satisfaction among unskilled auto workers is at the extreme low end of the scale; 84 percent would enter different occupations if they had a chance to choose, compared to 76 percent of blue-collar workers in general and 57 percent of white-collar workers who would do so. A 1965 study by Arthur Kornhauser *Mental Health of the Industrial Worker,* reported that 40 percent of his sample of auto-assembly-line workers had some symptoms of mental-health problems. These workers tended to be escapist or passive in their nonwork activities—they watched television, did not vote, and did not participate in community organizations.

Are these the social costs we must pay in order to lower prices to the consumer and increase profit percentages for stockholders? From the narrow, short-term viewpoint of the profit-and-loss statement, the answer is yes, but from the broader viewpoint of hard-core accountability, the answer is a resounding no. If all the economic and social costs involved in producing cars were added up, the price would be higher than what the consumer pays. It would include the costs of a decaying Detroit and the fact that it has the highest homicide rate in the country. These are considerations that engineers and shop superintendents are not inclined to take into account, but that modern chief executives must include in their planning and policy-making.

The highly touted job redesign efforts of Volvo and Saab in Sweden show that it is possible to show a concern for workers on the automobile assembly line. Management was spurred by the fact that few other nations have a labor force as small, highly educated, and comparatively prosperous as Sweden's. Consequently, it faced the consequences of job boredom earlier than did American factories, for in the mid-1960s, Sweden's labor turnover and absenteeism rates were running at rates almost double those of Detroit's.

In Saab's newly built engine-assembly factory near Stockholm, engines are now assembled by groups of four workers. Each group is given the 90 or so different parts needed and allowed to decide for themselves whether the four should work together to build a single engine, work in pairs, or individually. They must still, however, meet efficiency standards—the group must assemble four engines every 30 minutes. When Volvo's plant is completed, its 600 workers will be grouped in teams of 15–25 persons. They will produce entire chunks of the car under their own management and at their own pace.

The Saab and Volvo efforts at job redesign serve as models of how humanly destructive and socially damaging work arrangements can be altered when management makes up its mind to do so. Time will tell how much more consumers will have to pay for their cars. Time will also tell how much better the cars are. In any case, a principle of hard-core accountability that is rapidly gaining in acceptance is that the cost of a product should reflect all costs—social costs as well as ordinary production costs.

By eliminating or reducing social costs borne by employees, chief executives give concrete meaning to the show of concern that they have been accused of neglecting. As they make themselves visible through personal contact and the instruments of employee communications, chief executives are in a position to create the kind of cooperative atmosphere necessary for organizations to function effectively and efficiently.

The age of confrontation requires corporate chiefs to face up to a second challenge—the demand by a small, but publicly potent, minority of workers who seek to influence the social decisions of management. These employees see themselves as consumer advocates and socially conscious citizens. This role can obviously lead to direct conflict with corporate management and result in disloyalty to the company. Edward Gregory was an "evil" employee when he reported the failings of GM cars to Ralph Nader. Similarly, a B. F. Goodrich Co. engineer was an "evil" employee when he reported a falsification of military aircraft wheel and brake tests to the FBI. In both cases, the concern for producing safe, reliable products prevailed over the employee's loyalty to the boss and the company.

In the highly publicized case of the small group of black employees of Polaroid Corporation, we find a different motive operating. As members of a minority group and as citizens, they formed the Polaroid Revolutionary Workers Movement to force Polaroid to cease doing business in South Africa. The issue at stake is not only employees' right to speak out on public issues, but also whether there is justification for them to join in a concerted campaign to injure their employer through an organized boycott of its products.

As consumerism, racial discrimination, environmental protection, and other public issues capture the attention of a company's employees, they will mount pressure on their own employers to conform to new social values and expectations. The "rising wave of expectations" has become the "rising wave of demands." Chief executives thus become the targets of their own public statements and institutional ads proclaiming corporate citizenship and devotion to social responsibility.

The process may go even further, if the experience of university presidents is any indication. They were expected to reflect new social and political values not only by revising internal policies, but also by using the power of the university to change public policy on such issues as civil rights, the war in Vietnam, corporate power, ecology, and the environment. The "politics of confrontation" of SDS and other extremists extended beyond the goal of satisfying immediate grievances to the destruction of authority itself. Some alumni of the 1964 Berkeley riots and others in the late 1960s are now corporate employees. The chief executive can't help wondering whether these alumni have placed their social idealism behind them or whether their devotion to social causes will erupt as disloyalty to their companies.

Ralph Nader has clearly stated his view. He proposes a "whistle blowing" tactic whereby any person in any organization who feels that a decision by company superiors harms society would disclose such information to a "public interest" organization. Responsibility to society, Nader says, transcends responsibility to an employer.

James M. Roche, Chairman of General Motors, probably reflects the feelings of all chief executives when he reacted with the following statement: "Some of the enemies of business now encourage an employee to be disloyal to the enterprise. They want to create suspicion and disharmony and pry into the proprietary interests of the business. However this is labelled —industrial espionage, whistle blowing or professional responsibility—it is another tactic for spreading disunity and creating conflict."

Traditionally, the employer could fire an employee who leaked confidential company information. According to common law, an employer's right to discharge was absolute, and even today this principle is generally upheld by the courts as a necessary means to enforce individual plant discipline and maintain loyalty. But statutory and collective bargaining incursions over the years have severely limited this right. Increasingly, employees are protected against discharge for exercising those personal rights which have no legitimate connection with the employment relationship. The courts are likely to let employees exercise their rights of free speech in public controversy involving their employer. Also, the climate of public opinion will also back them up and severely limit the company's freedom of action.

Even if the possibility of firing an employee were not so restricted, this negative reaction is more likely to be inappropriate to the nature of the problem. The point is that employees seek a voice in guiding some of the affairs of the companies they work for. Only a few employees are now interested in the company's social policies, but their numbers will grow. Major attention will still be given to matters that concern them directly, and they will want a greater voice in determining the conditions under which they work.

In either case, employees who feel frustrated and powerless within their organizations turn to outside groups—the union, a social-action group or government—to help them. In Europe employees have sought more formal means of control—

work councils or membership on the board of directors—as is illustrated by the recent expansion of codetermination in Germany. Both American and European trends carry a clear message for chief executives: their estrangement from their employees cannot continue. Within the limits of their time, corporate chiefs must make themselves not only more visible, but also more responsive to employee grievances, feelings, and aspirations.

The solution lies in the improvement of upward communications. Like water, information and ideas do not flow upward by themselves; some pumping mechanisms are needed. Dan H. Fenn, Jr., and Daniel Yankelovich listed a variety of such devices in a recent *Harvard Business Review* article. Among them were these: counsellors or ombudsmen, either employee-elected or management-appointed, to present grievances to top management; special "councils," somewhat modeled after European work councils, where managers and/or employees get together to discuss problems of mutual interest; middle-management and lower-level junior boards of directors to make policy recommendations to the corporate board.

None of these systems of upward communications is effective unless relevant matters can reach the very top. Dissenting opinions as well as recommendations made by the majority should be included in reports that reach the chief executive. Indeed, the top executive should sit in on some of the meetings of a junior board of directors and meet with senior ombudsmen. Through personal involvement, the chief executive demonstrates concern for employees and provides the essential assurance that the system is responsive. He often finds the "evil" employee to be merely human.

9
Consumerism

Nothing is more vital to the success of the chief executive than sales and profits. Practically every letter "To Our Stockholders" in annual reports begins with a reference to sales and profits. For example, U. S. Steel's 1973 letter by Edgar B. Speer, chairman of the board, starts with: "U. S. Steel had record shipments and sales during 1973." The top line of every P & L statement, of course, begins with sales and revenues. Whatever production, financial, or other problems may exist, they tend to evaporate in the sunlight of healthy sales and profit figures.

Whereas profits are uppermost on the chief executive's mind, consumerism is somewhere on the bottom. Our questionnaire findings indicate that only 13 percent of the chief executives would bother speaking to a consumerist spokesman. To gain the executive's attention, there would have to be a crisis, such as a condemnation of a product by the FDA, FTC, or some other governmental agency. This impression is supported by Frederick E. Webster's recent survey, which was published by the *Harvard Business Review*. Three hundred forty-three Fortune 500 companies didn't even bother to respond to this consumerism survey; of those who did reply, fewer than a dozen reported planned, coordinated consumerism programs.

The chief executive's reactions appear defensive and reveal a widespread ignorance of the basic nature of consumerism. We can accuse the corporate chief of issue avoidance, because 14 percent of the chief executives had this trait; this neglect of consumerism is probably based on the belief of the company's limited responsibility to consumers.

Too many chief executives and their marketing vice-presidents treat a sale like a one-shot sexual encounter. There must be a reason for *caveat emptor* to have become such a cliche for this kind of affair. The risk is almost entirely on the side of the buyer. The cresting wave of consumerism is the signal that buyers are no longer willing to be the victims and that it may well be *caveat vendor.*

It's best to think of consumers as wives, not mistresses. Consumers want a sale to amount to a marriage—the beginning, not the end, of a relationship. Like the economist who describes consumption as a "flow of services," consumers like to find continuing satisfaction in the products they buy. The seller must "serve" the customer and not be content with merely "selling" to them, for serving people is the ultimate purpose of business. If a company succeeds in doing this, it not only makes a profit; it passes society's most critical test of whether it will survive.

The issue of consumerism is a warning to the chief executive that business is flunking the test. As consumers, people are saying that product performance is not measuring up to product expectations. The gap between performance and expectations has grown so wide that consumers have revolted, and their purchasing revolt has become a social movement. More than sales and profits are at stake. The free enterprise system itself is also on trial, for the marketplace is the symbol of our economic system. Without a doubt, the current low level of public confidence in business can be attributed largely to the malfunctioning of the traditional marketing function.

Chief executives should not make the mistake of viewing consumerism as just another of those pesky social problems that divert their attention from more important business problems. Consumerism strikes at the heart of business—producing and marketing the company's products. Consumerism can't be handled in a quarantining fashion by simply creating a new vice-presidency to listen to consumer complaints. Chief executives must see to it that there is feedback to everybody in the company who deals with products.

Products must be designed to satisfy consumer wants, manufactured to meet acceptable standards, sold to informed customers, and where relevant, serviced throughout the life of the product. A chief executive's orientation must not be narrowly limited to only one point in this process—making the sale—but must be broadened to include the total spectrum of the seller-buyer relationship. Only by accepting responsibility for design, production, marketing, and servicing does the chief executive meet the expectations of the consumers and the obligations of hard-core accountability.

At the focal point of this extended seller-buyer relationship is the marketplace. What most consumerists complain about is that the advantage in this relationship lies almost completely with the seller. The seller is "in the know"; the consumer is not. To the consumer, "seller" equals "company president." This is not, however, the way the chief executive sees it—or at least talks about it. To the chief executive, "the consumer is king," and companies have no choice but to obey every customer's every wish and whim.

Anybody who looks at company economic education materials soon realizes that business leaders really want to believe that the world of Adam Smith actually exists—that there are many buyers and sellers who compete against one another and thereby, through the "invisible hand," protect the public interest. Businessmen also like to make the convenient assumption that consumers are well informed and know what they're doing. This would mean that they understand their own needs and preferences, are aware of the existence of every product and its price, and can put all this information together to "maximize their utility."

Chief executives call these assumptions realities. That's the danger of the corporate view of the marketplace. Consumers then want companies to live up to their own description of the ideal model. This model underlies the four basic rights contained in the late President Kennedy's Consumer Bill of Rights—the right to be informed, the right to safety, the right to choose, and the right to be heard.

The right to be informed is one of the key demands of consumerists. This sounds reasonable enough, but most chief executives don't yet seem ready to accede to this demand. They cling to the principle that consumers should beware and take it upon themselves to obtain reliable product information. An increasing number of consumers do indeed seek product information. About 1,500,000 people subscribe to *Consumer Reports*, and twice as many more read it. Other guides are also available: *Consumers' Research Magazine, Consumers Digest,* and *The Consumers' Guide to Better Buying.* In that much-heralded era of two-way cable television, subscribers will supposedly have ready access to even more product information. But it is a safe bet that 95 percent of the public—and particularly those with low incomes—will not be willing or able to buy this information. If impulse buying is a major factor in marketing, where's the opportunity or access for reliable information on any given product? So, although chief executives might feel exonerated, informational grievances will not be eliminated, and consumers eventually will pressure the government for action.

The consumerism issue becomes a classical dilemma for chief executives. Should they resist change through stalling action, or should they respond to change through voluntary action? If they choose to resist, they invite government intervention—that's the plain lesson of economic history. What they can expect is at least three forms of government action. One form is legislation, and the 28 consumer-protection laws passed since 1962 that are now in effect are ample evidence of the willingness of Congress to act in behalf of the consumer. A second form is direct government service to consumers, by providing them with the information needed. And a third form is to enforce existing legislation more stringently.

Many chief executives are devoting more attention to consumer bills under consideration by stepping up their public affairs efforts. As the packing industry learned with the Fair Packaging and Labeling Act of 1966, it is better for industry leaders to discuss their problems with legislators than to refuse to change or to deride the demand for change as a threat to the free-enterprise system. By cooperating, the resulting act emphasizes self-regulation rather than government restrictions and gave the packing industry 18 months in which to establish its own standards.

With regard to direct government provision of product in-formation to consumers, little has been done so far, and what has been provided is mainly of symbolic value. For example, a Consumer Product Information Coordinating Center, estab-lished in 1970, published an index of 200 selected government publications which tell consumers how to buy, use, and take care of consumer products. It includes some controversial pub-lications, such as the results of comparative government brand-name testing of hearing aids. This information, long de-manded by consumer groups, was until recently withheld by the government. Many chief executives have thus been lulled into a false sense of security.

Most of the information now provided by the government is simply a by-product of its research, development, and procure-ment activities. But in the future, the government could go the way of Sweden and establish its own testing laboratories for consumer products and institutes for informative labeling. Such a development in this country would run counter to the histori-cal establishment of private and independent testing labora-tories, such as the Underwriters Laboratories, founded in 1894. Unless impetus is given to the formation of more private testing laboratories and the public disclosure of results, industry can expect more government activity in this area.

A more immediate problem facing chief executives is the third form of government intervention—enforcing existing reg-ulations, particularly with regard to so-called deceptive adver-tising. We know from our survey that chief executives would view strong condemnation by the FTC as a major crisis. And well they should if integrity is the number-one quality they seek not only in hiring executives, but also in their corporate image. They cannot escape personal responsibility for they must surely be aware of their companies' national advertising campaigns. We see from our survey that they are alert watchers of TV news programs and readers of newspapers and magazines dealing with business.

Their peril has become greater since the FTC instituted its new policy toward advertising—that all major industries must provide substantive data in support of their advertising claims. Large companies are more affected than small ones. The FTC was apparently convinced by Ralph Nader's statement that the country's largest companies can do greater harm because they reach the greatest number of people by mass media advertising. Previously, the FTC went after small, fly-by-night outfits, thinking them to be the most vicious and harmful.

What's in store for companies can be seen in the FTC charges against Hi-C and Wonder Bread. Although charges were dropped after three years, the FTC contended in the Hi-C case that the advertising claim that it was high in Vitamin C was misleading. Its argument was that the amount of this vitamin was not really extraordinary when compared to natural fruit juice. The question was what the word "extraordinary" means.

In the Wonder Bread case, the FTC accused the Continental Baking Co. and its advertising agency, Ted Bates & Co., for falsely advertising Wonder Bread as an extraordinary food for producing dramatic growth in children. Building on the theme "Helps Build Strong Bodies 12 Ways," a television commercial time sequence depicted a young child growing to a 12-year-old while a voice-over video told parents how they could help by serving Wonder Bread to their children. Was this an imaginative, dramatic way of showing the nutritional value of fortified bread, or was it, as the FTC charged, a case of deceptive advertising?

Late in 1974, milk advertising came under fire from the FTC, which denied milk marketers' claims that milk is good for everyone.

For the chief executive, the question again becomes "What consitutes corporate lying?" As the keeper of the corporate conscience and builder of the company's moral code, the corporate chief must take a stand on what advertising is acceptable. The CEO can't claim to be a person of integrity or expect the public to trust the company and its products if they judge company advertising to be false, deceptive, or just plain stupid.

The chief executive and the advertising staff have to decide on the proper balance between truth and fancy. Expressed in cold, objective terms, truth may take the extreme of a "tombstone ad" that the SEC so long mandated as appropriate for advertising securities. Even members of the dismal science of economics and consumer activists would at least favor a step in the direction of fancy by holding up the Sears catalog as a model of informative yet attractive advertising. Most Americans, however, want to see and hear advertising that is more enjoyable and imaginative.

Like poets, people in the advertising fraternity are granted the license to create symbols that show the full possibilities of a product that would otherwise be buried under the weight of heavy, dull facts. Products come alive when their uses and resulting satisfaction to the consumer are dramatized. They take on interesting dimensions when the photographer's lens helps reshape reality, as fashion ads do by lengthening women's legs to fit a basketball player's body. Since people know what people really look like, these liberties are accepted cheerfully. But when sandpaper instead of bristling whiskers are shaved on television commercials, that becomes fakery. People have no reality check for this kind of trick.

Ray Bauer's study *Advertising in America* shows that next to the repetitive, monotonous, and interrupting nature of some advertising, what people find most offensive is untruthfulness and exaggeration. People might be deceived and as a result waste their time and money and perhaps risk their health. So although people don't object to some puffery in advertising for the sake of enjoyment, they do draw the line at the point where they believe they are being taken advantage of.

Unfortunately, offending companies often benefit by making exaggerated advertising claims. Like Gresham's law, the bad drives out the good, for competitors must either adopt the same practices or commit economic suicide. The long-run harm done to themselves and to business as a whole is ignored. For this reason, joint action through self-regulation or FTC policing is needed. Self-regulation can go a long way toward removing counterproductive and socially harmful practices. A step in this direction has now been taken by the Association of National Advertisers through the establishment of the National Advertising Review Board. Its purpose is to consider complaints of unethical or deceptive advertising. If the complaint has merit, attempts are made to convince the company involved to remove the objectionable ad. When private remedies fail, the matter is referred to the FTC. Experience with a similar type of review board in Sweden shows that this form of self-regulation can be highly effective.

The chief executive should encourage these moves toward self-regulation in the hope that the evolving professional norms and standards will eliminate consumer complaints about deceptive advertising. The corporate chief must also prod advertising, sales, public relations, and other communications executives into working out an integrated policy of consumer information. And as a member of the television audience, the top executive should monitor his company's advertising and respond sharply when it is out of line with personal standards of truth.

Although product information deserves major attention, the chief executive must also consider policies and practices that affect other aspects of consumerism. These are the processes that precede the sale of products—product design and manufacturing. Many chief executives still believe in planned obsolescence for autos and durable goods. James M. Roche, former chairman of GM, expressed this belief when he said: "Planned obsolescence, in my opinion, is another word for progress." He's right, of course, when the product improvements are substantial. But he's dead wrong when "progress" means the premature wearing out of a flimsily built product or superficial improvements and frills. One of the lessons of the ecology movement and the era of energy and materials shortages we have entered is that we need to conserve. One of the best ways of doing that is to design and make products that last.

A foreign automobile manufacturer is now designing a car that will last 20 years. Profit can still be made by charging a higher price for these cars and by placing greater emphasis on the adjunct service industry for preventive maintenance and repairs. Other auto manufacturers are designing cars with built-in self-diagnostic devices, so that owners and mechanics can detect worn out brakes and malfunctions. Chief executives in these companies have gone beyond considering consumerism as a problem. To them, it is an opportunity for product and marketing innovations.

Corrections in product design and manufacturing are more likely to be made when there is adequate customer feedback. For this reason, many chief executives are paying more attention to the postpurchase phase of sales. "Hot lines"—special toll-free phones at company headquarters so that customers can register complaints—have been set up by Whirlpool, Chrysler, and other companies. To achieve their full benefit, however, these feedback systems must relay the collected information to those points in the organization where corrections should be made.

How this is done is illustrated by Ford's "We listen Better" program. First, each letter of complaint is answered with a personalized letter. At the end of a year, 1,000,000 letters had been handled. Equally important is that the nature of the request or complaint is recorded and summarized. It was estimated that about 45 percent of the letters dealt with requests for information; 33 percent, with current production problems. When a major problem was identified, this information was referred to the production department, where actual improvements in product design and manufacture could be made.

General Foods, in its "quality assurance program," has a similar internal-feedback system. Once a week, full reports on incoming product complaints are sent to each product division, along with samples of any defective products. In 1971 alone, the company received 114,000 letters from consumers.

At Motorola, some executives become personally involved in their "consumer satisfaction" program. Whenever the vice-president and general manager of the Consumer Products Division travels about the country on business, he visits the homes of some Quasar color television owners. His intention is to learn in a face-to-face situation if customers are fully satisfied with their purchase. Wouldn't it be dramatic if a chief executive occasionally showed this kind of interest?

What consumerists want most of all in the postpurchase phase of consumer relations is improved warranties that show that the company really stands behind its products. A good example is American Motors' "Buyer Protection Plan." Owners are promised virtually "no questions asked" repairs on anything during the first year or 12,000 miles. They are offered a further option, at $149, that includes two years or 24,000 miles of total coverage, including routine maintenance. The Sears policy of "bring-it-back-we'll-change-it" has been a significant factor in that company's continuing sales volume, Sears executives affirm.

In all of these case studies, the lesson is that the entire organization responds to the consumer. Indeed, this is the only appropriate response to the consumer movement. If consumerism is treated like some sort of disease, to be isolated and battened down, it will simply break out in more severe form at a later time. But if the corporate head regards it as a flag from a key public that there's trouble with a product, the whole organization can be whipped into line.

The chief executive is the only corporate officer who can mobilize all the parts of the organization to effect a total response to new consumer expectations. The CEO must show a commitment to the goals of consumerism by indicating displeasure at the appropriate time. It doesn't take much—just a frown or a long look. The boss has got to want to do it and must insist on necessary product redesign, better quality control, informative and truthful advertising, and postpurchase satisfaction.

If consumers are satisfied with their purchases, the company and the economic system pass society's ultimate test—serving people. If this is accomplished, these same people will be favorably disposed to becoming stockholders, employees, and supporters of the free enterprise system.

10
Crisis in energy and materials

Like dinosaurs, chief executives in the oil industry stand in real danger of extinction—unless they can adapt to their suddenly changed environment. Other chief executives should observe their plight, for inevitably they, too, will face the same set of conditions.

Once the largest, most terrifying animals that ever stalked the earth, the dinosaurs are extinct because they had become cemented into a specific environment. When the terrain, climate, and vegetation changed, they could not adjust. Biologists thereby draw the conclusion that survival depends on adaptability—a lesson that applies to the human animal as well.

Chief executives are a breed that historically excelled in their ability to adjust. They perceived changes before others did and profited by innovating new products and technology. Now, chief executives are cast in the opposite role of behaving like the dinosaurs, intransigent and stubbornly resistant to change.

The old environment faced by the oil industry was dominated by engineering and economic considerations. Although these remain, the new environment emphasizes ecological and political factors. These shifts in environmental conditions have been taking place so gradually as to be almost imperceptible. But now, the energy crisis, like an earthquake, shows the new ecological and political terrain in clear profile. It has given us a preview of the doomsday that ecologists have prophesized and a dress rehearsal of the chief executive's performance in the public arena.

For years, ecologists have been warning us that we cannot continue to gobble up the earth's resources at ever-increasing rates, for the earth is a spaceship with limited supplies. What is needed, they said, is conservation of energy and materials and an acceptance of a thriftier life style.

The Arab oil embargo, although a political rather than a natural phenomenon, suddenly brought about the specter of doomsday—long lines of drivers waiting for gas, volatile tempers, low home temperatures, factory shut-downs, and ever-rising prices. But people didn't think so much about ecology as they did about the oil companies that had failed them. Resulting unfavorable public opinion led to powerful domestic political pressures and demands for governmental intervention. As prices of gasoline, home heating fuel, and electricity rose—often drastically—the public realized that they were facing a grim turn of events. They were told by both company executives and government officials that the age of cheap power was gone forever. Along with news of high food prices and other shortages, Americans were facing a fall in their real standard of living. Getting used to affluence was easy, but giving it up by accepting a new life style with fewer material goods was difficult.

It has become a feature of our American civilization that when its people don't want to face up to economic realities, they turn to the government for salvation. They didn't have to try hard when the energy crisis began, because most politicians were all too willing to espouse the cause of cheap gasoline for everyone. By upholding the economic aspirations of their constituents, their bias was toward finding short-term political remedies rather than long-term economic solutions. For example, some congressmen favored rationing as a way to keep prices down and to equitably distribute available supplies. They did not sufficiently consider the increased exploration costs of obtaining new supplies.

These domestic political developments were matched by growing foreign political forces. The "third world"—the less-developed countries in Africa, Asia, and Latin America—were learning to unite and restrict supplies, thereby extracting monopolistic prices. The Organization of Petroleum Exporting Countries (OPEC) scored the first major victory with its successful oil embargo. Its control over oil supplies was used not only for economic gain, but also for achieving its Middle East political aims. The OPEC serves as an awesome model for other nations to follow.

Chief executives in many industries now realize that our growing dependency on foreign sources of supply for an increasing proportion of our natural resources will increase our vulnerability to foreign political and economic pressures in the future. A recent announcement by the Interior Department supports this fear, for it states that the United States already depends on imports for more than half its supply of six of 13 basic raw materials—aluminum, chromium, manganese, nickel, tin, and zinc. Conditions would get worse by 1985, when we would also depend on imports for more than half of our iron, lead, and tungsten; by the year 2000, copper, potassium, and sulphur would be added to that list.

How should chief executives respond to these new developments in what has become known as the politics of scarcity? For their part, the oil company presidents and chairmen sought to preserve free enterprise, with its immutable law of supply and demand, which had handled the problem of scarcity so marvelously over the centuries. With higher prices, they thought optimistically, it would be possible to bore deeper into the earth's crust, probe the ocean depths, and forge new technological breakthroughs. The problem of scarcity could thereby be licked and the ecological forebodings of the doomsday prophets proved wrong.

But they would have to convince the public and the government that higher prices were in the public interest. A public communications campaign was undertaken with the basic theme that "adequate prices are an essential incentive to encourage greater search for new oil and gas reserves," a theme expressed as early as 1964 in the annual report of the Phillips Petroleum Company. In 1971 alone, six of the largest firms—Exxon, Shell, Amoco,

Gulf, Mobil, and Texaco—spent more than $110 million on institutional advertising.

When the crisis occurred in October 1973, this campaign was sharply accelerated. To Russell Baker of the *New York Times*, the new effort appeared like a Madison Avenue promotion: "The new miracle energy crisis with XP–87 for businesses too timid to raise prices without twice as much economic excuse power." Some new theme appeared during the first few months of the energy crisis, as seen in the following excerpts:

- There's talk around that the energy shortage is contrived. It's not. It's real. (Exxon, October 17, 1973)

- Atlantic Richfield finds no solace in the fact that for years we and others have warned of the perils to our nation's well-being of this dependence on foreign oil. (November 16, 1973)

- Long lead times—often five to eight years—are required for the development of major new energy supplies . . . Because of the long lead time, we should begin work immediately on ways of solving our long-term energy needs. (Continental Oil Company, November 16, 1973)

- What you do to save energy is what counts now . . . Even an all-out energy-saving program may not be enough. But it will help keep demand in closer balance with the available supply. (Exxon, November 21, 1973)

The strategy behind these public communication efforts was both defensive and offensive. Defensively, oil company presidents and chairmen know that polls showed that the majority of Americans believed that the energy crisis was contrived by the oil companies to get higher prices—as well as for other reasons, such as getting congressional approval for the Alaskan pipeline. Offensively, they wanted to step up their pre-energy crisis campaign to gain public support for a free-enterprise solution to growing energy demands. This meant maximum freedom for oil companies to operate within the economic system with a minimum of governmental interference.

But they faced setbacks in executing their strategy. Although the oil company chief executives preferred to remain anonymous figures behind the curtain of the impersonal economic system, the politics of scarcity forced them into the center of the public arena. The Senate Government Operations Subcommittee started an inquisition of the oil industry in January 1974. Officers of the nation's seven biggest oil companies, sitting side by side at a long table in the same marble chamber where Watergate witnesses were grilled, were sworn to tell the truth. "The American people want to know," Senator Henry Jackson explained, "why the prices of home heating oil and gasoline have doubled when the companies report record high inventories and stocks." He accusingly demanded to know "if this so-called energy crisis is only a pretext, a cover to eliminate the major source of price competition—the independents —to raise prices, to repeal environmental laws and to force adoption of new tax subsidies." Harry Bridges, president of Shell Oil Co., Z. D. Bonner, president of the Gulf Oil Company, and other top officers were now personally experiencing the age of confrontation.

The American public, which had seldom seen or heard any of the heads of our country's largest corporations, could now turn on their television sets and watch Z. D. Bonner defend the innocence of the oil industry. Bonner talked about three mistaken notions concerning the energy shortage: "First is the notion that the Arabs are to blame for the United States' energy crisis. Second is the mistaken notion that the United States' energy resources are about to be exhausted. And, third, the notion that the diabolical major oil companies contrived to produce shortage so they can make greater profits."

Then, in 1974, when profits for 1973 were reported by the major oil companies, chief executives faced a new public relations problem—how to justify record high profits while the country was making sacrifices. Exxon, the largest in the business, made 59 percent higher profits than in 1972—$2.44 billion—the largest net income ever reported by an American company. Exxon held a press conference, believed to be the first ever held by the company on earnings, to describe how it had accumulated its profits and how it intended to use them. People could see J. K. Jamieson, Exxon chairman, insist that he wasn't "embarrassed" by the spectacular jump in 1973 earnings: "We aren't making windfall profits," he asserted.

Unfortunately, the White House didn't help the oil industry's public posture on profits. In a nationwide radio address, President Nixon proclaimed that "private profiteering at the expense of public sacrifice must never be tolerated in a free country . . . Too many Americans have sacrificed too much to allow this to happen."

To defuse public criticism of oil company profits, a new theme appeared in institutional ads. "How in all conscience can anyone call these excess profits?" asked H. Bridges, president of Shell Oil, in a full-page ad in the *New York Times*, which he reportedly wrote himself. But nowhere in the ad could a simply stated profit figure be found. "We still do not know our results for the 4th quarter of 1973," the ad said. In a confusion of graphs and statistics, the closest the ad came to stating a profit figure was for the first nine months of 1973. Income during this period, according to the ad, "would have had to be 38% or $97 million higher to equal the 1968 return on investment." Unfortunately for the CEOs of the oil companies, a great deal of publicity attended the high increase in profits during 1974. It was as a follow-up to this ridiculously confusing disclosure that the ad stated: "How, in all conscience, this profit performance can be described as 'reaping windfall profits from the energy crisis' escapes my comprehension."

This is precisely the kind of double-talk that Irving Kristol decried in a *Wall Street Journal* article entitled "The Credibility of Corporations." He accused the oil industry of engaging in "clever public relations" and thereby losing the battle for candor and credibility. "What is one to make of a corporation," he asked, "which proudly announces that it has just completed the most profitable year in its history—and then simultaneously declares that its return on capital is pitifully inadequate, that it is suffering from a terrible cost-squeeze, etc., etc.,?"

The problem, however, is not that the oil industry engaged

in clever public relations, but that its chief executives failed to understand that public relations require a company to operate in the public interest—and not only as the corporation chooses to define it. Making a reasonable profit is certainly in the public interest. It must be high enough to satisfy stockholders, attract new capital, and provide the basis for future growth. The need to make a profit is uncontestable, for the public interest is also promoted.

But the oil industry overstated its case. Its chief executives proclaimed that without the profit incentive, they could not explore for new sources of oil, build new refineries, and market their products. Unfortunately, the public impression is that the oil companies are totally unwilling to lift a finger in overcoming the fuel shortage unless their own profit demands are fully met.

Pointing out that a certain return on investment is needed to accumulate and attract the enormous capital required to exploit new sources of energy is one thing. But saying that the only incentive for business cooperation is profits doesn't show much respect or concern for the public interest. No wonder that the public image of the oil industry is that of a hungry, rapacious, greedy tiger. This image is compounded by the nature of the product sold. Its "essentiality" in a modern industrial nation, particularly one as motorized as ours, gives it one of the attributes of a public utility. The public therefore expects the oil industry to put the public interest before any other goal; profits are simply a means of providing public service. The way the oil company chief executives talked and acted, it seemed as if these priorities were reversed.

Another way in which oil company executives appeared to be working against the public interest was by withholding information from the government. The "rights of privacy" were overemphasized in the context of the emergency nature of the energy crisis. The Federal Energy Office and the Congress obviously had an urgent "need to know" if they were to handle the emergency allocation program and draft a national energy policy. Senator William Proxmire, chairman of the Joint Economic Committee, contended that the data Mr. Simon's energy office got from petroleum refiners represented only about 10 percent of the oil information it needed. The industry's unwillingness to disclose information was evidenced earlier in their negative reaction to a questionnaire from Senator Jackson. The most uncooperative company was Exxon, which refused to answer a single question, on grounds that the information was "proprietary"—and that included the number of gas stations the company owned.

Exxon's excuse that certain information is proprietary appeared highly unconvincing in the new context of chronic shortages. Claims that the oil business is highly competitive simply didn't seem to square with reality. The effect of denying information to the Federal Energy Office and legislative bodies goes beyond creating a bad public image; there is an intimate connection between the willingness to disclose information and the ability to earn public trust. In a simple matter, such as holding an open house when moving into a new community, this connection is readily recognized. Yet it was seemingly ignored at a time of angry public opinion and low public confidence in big business. In such a context, the stance of secrecy is essentially a "public be damned" act that destroys the trust which constitutes the social fabric of society.

It was difficult for the American public to avoid the impression that the oil industry placed its own welfare above the public interest and that its chief executives were exceedingly selfish and arrogant. Viewers who watched *The Advocates* debate on a Federal Oil Corporation could hear John Swearingen, chairman of Standard Oil of Indiana, treat Senator Fred Harris like a schoolboy. Swearingen kept making statements such as: "I don't think you know what you're talking about"; "Now just a minute. I'm trying to educate you"; and "I hope you understand what I told you."

No *mea culpa* was, of course, ever heard from the oil industry except for the slight admission that demand for energy was underestimated. Even the Arabs, in a full-page ad, showed a spark of compassion by acknowledging their role in the energy shortage. In an "Open letter to the American people," Omar Sakkar, Saudi Arabia's Minister of Foreign Affairs said on January 3, 1974: "We, the Arabs, wish you a Happy New Year.

Your holiday season may have been marred by the hardships of the energy crisis. Ours is haunted by the threat of death and continued aggression. But it is not in bitterness that we address this message to you, and it is our hope that there will be no bitterness in you as you read it."

It was more than a lack of humanity and touch of humility that accounted for the failure of company presidents and other oil company executives to win over the American people. They had to analyze their own basic attitudes toward the public and make some quick readjustments if they were to avoid the fate of the dinosaur. The crisis had enabled the oil companies to take their case before the American people. Now, the crisis could cause irrevocable damage to the industry, for people and some of their congressmen were in the mood for drastic action. The stakes couldn't be higher, for failure to win public confidence could result in price controls, excess profits taxes, the removal of tax benefits, and if the game was really lost, nationalization of the industry. In a sense, the whole free-enterprise system was on trial.

To regain public confidence in themselves and the free-enterprise system, oil industry executives—and company presidents and chairmen elsewhere—would have to reconsider their "public philosophy," a term used by Walter Lippman to describe how much weight leaders should give to the voice of public opinion relative to the opinions of experts in policy formation. The chief executive who listens to experts exclusively or primarily expresses a belief in elitism—that those people who are "the best and the brightest" and armed with facts should dominate. Elitism also welcomes the opinions of those select persons who hold special responsibilities in society, such as the managers of enterprises. The chief executive who gives public opinion the major weight in decisions, by contrast, reflects the public philosophy of popularism—that everybody's opinion counts. This is the democratic ideal and it also supports the universal law of politics that no government can long endure without the consent of the governed. The modern dilemma facing chief executives is that while decisions become more complex and require expert opinion, the pressures for greater participatory democracy are also rising. It is the responsibility of chief executives to decide how much weight to give to each side on a particular policy matter.

The experience of the Kennedy and Johnson administrations certainly shows that excessive reliance on expert presidential advisers can lead to such disasters as the Bay of Pigs fiasco and the Vietnam war. Part of the problem—for the president of the United States and the chief executive of a major company—is deciding which experts to listen to and making sure that "groupthink" doesn't snuff out opposing views. But the larger problem is deciding what role public opinion should be allowed to play.

The public philosophy of oil industry chief executives was all too apparent in their air of superiority and the mantle of economic elitism they chose to adorn themselves with. Only they knew the facts and, in the spirit of Boulwareism, only they knew what was in the balanced best interests of the public. The long-standing suspicion that the oil industry ran the State Department's Middle East foreign policy seemed only too true as this arrogant elitist attitude was displayed in domestic affairs.

Every affected special interest has a right, if not an obligation, to make its views known on a matter of public policy. The oil industry certainly did this with its prescription for the energy crisis—to deregulate price controls of natural gas, continue and increase depletion allowances, use tax money for a Manhattan-type project to develop new energy sources, temporarily suspend or permanently lower environmental standards, and create an economic climate that will provide the immense capital (and profits) needed to develop energy resources. Much of this prescription is indeed based on extensive knowledge of technical and economic facts gained from long experience in the oil industry. Their legitimate claim to expertise cannot be denied by the oil-producing nations, the American government, or the American people.

But elements other than expertise enter into the making of a national energy policy. The public philosophy of chief executives cannot be solely elitist. Room for a popularist philosophy must also be made, for not only technical and scientific facts, but also human values are an ingredient of public policy. No matter how illogical or idealist these values may appear to hard-nosed business executives, they must be encompassed in their public philosophy.

This public philosophy must be embedded in the ultimate frame of reference for executive behavior—the relationship of business to society and government. One major change in these relationships is especially threatening as a result of the energy crisis and the impending materials shortage. This is the move toward a managed economy. Hints have already been dropped by Herbert Stein, former chairman of the President's Council of Economic Advisors, that some form of national planning, comparable to France's, is needed to cope with today's economic and political problems.

The energy shortage holds the most fearsome threat to business, because energy resources underlie all economic activity. Hence, the power to allocate fuel gives the FEO director the authority to decide what products companies, industries, and whole regions can produce, and at what level. Under the guise of fuel allocation, the government's will could be enforced on a whole range of economic and political issues.

Chief executives of leading corporations, particularly in the oil industry, have to face up to their new environment, one in which production and economic considerations by themselves no longer guarantee survival. They must not assume that the price mechanism or the automatic workings of the free-enterprise system will safeguard the public interest. Chief executives have entered the public domain and must consciously strive to balance the often conflicting claims of profits and the public interest. By accepting a more enlightened public philosophy, they have a chance of survival.

IV

BEFORE AND AFTER

11
Ident-i-kit portrait
of a president

Who is the chief executive? What does he do? How does he act?
What are his hobbies? Would we want him as a neighbor?
What's he really like?

Throughout this book we've dealt with the president,
chairman, or chief executive as some faceless nonperson in-
habiting a title. Now the time has come to put it together—to
add up all the discrete units and, like Dr. Frankenstein, see
what we have.

In any computation of survey analyses, there are always
dominant, tonic, and modal results. From our survey we found
the chief executive to be a definitely describable man with
positive and negative characteristics, traits, and habits. Here he
is, then.

- Our chief executive is between 45 and 65 years of age. His
  marriage has been eminently successful, insofar as he's
  been wedded to the same wife his whole life of sex part-
  nership (88 percent versus the national marriage/success
  ratio of 67 percent). But unlike most other Americans, he
  has 2.87 children versus the national average of 1.9.

- Religion plays a role in his life, since he's a regular
  church-goer.

- The corporate chief is only half sold on owning a second
  home. And, when it comes to the automobile which he

owns personally, as opposed to the company car, it's usually a luxury job.

- The company head is a man of integrity and a believer in accepting responsibility. Astonishingly, he is neither curious nor ingenious. He does not admire boldness; nor, on the other hand, does he practice prudence.

- A reliable man, the corporate chief approves strongly of those who get things started and those who get things done.

- Naturally, as a leader, the chief executive has exhibited drive and creativity, and he agrees that leaders ought to be both perceptive and enthusiastic.

- However, the CEO finds it difficult to be articulate or communicative and is quite tepid about the desirability of imagination in a chief executive. He doesn't think that the ability to concentrate is particularly important, either.

- Getting along with peers, superiors, or subordinates does not greatly concern the chief executive, who thinks that getting along with business associates is not a strong suit in the game to get to the top.

Our emerging personality portrait would be incomplete without "warts."

- We find that the chief corporate officer is impatient, opinionated, and intolerant of failure. Although he's not arrogant, he is egotistical, a perfectly common trait of top leaders. Whether one needs a generous helping of egotism to become the head of any group, or whether the ego fattens into significance once one has achieved the summit will always be argued by psychologists.

- The corporate chief is close-mouthed—even secretive— unemotional, and impersonal. These qualities, together with his cold objectivity, give him an autocratic and dictatorial manner.

- Although he might be expected to take care of his relatives in his company, they'd better not count on it, as he is definitely not nepotistic.

● Amazingly, the CEO will avoid confrontation over issues. Perhaps he feels so secure that he can disregard such confrontations. More likely, as one who has made it to the top against ferocious competition, the chief executive knows enough not to go into battle unless he's certain of winning, for frequent losses subtract substantively from authority.

Every person bears some residue of each environment he or she has traversed; any significant contact with another entity results in some exchange of qualities—it gives dimension. Our president, chairman, or chief executive shares this characteristic with all other people, but to a greater degree. So, although our portrait reveals the chief executive as a generalist, he has a marked penchant for finance and is also fairly strong as in marketing. But concomitant with the corporate chief's eschewing of "getting along with others" is his lack of feeling in labor-employee relations.

Our chief executive is not a production type, nor does he find the law irresistible. In an area in which one would expect a certain healthy complexion—public relations—the corporate head is as bereft as he is of labor-employee concerns.

What does concern the chief executive, though, is inflation and the energy crisis. He gives these two matters top priority among his business problems. They provide another perspective for this profile.

The survey's typical chief executive is a good listener and a quick study. He pays attention when someone speaks to him, and he absorbs and retains full oral presentations much better than most people do. He's also able to comprehend and absorb complex written reports and programs with easy confidence.

The chief executive we're describing projects an appearance of candor and truthfulness, even under the pressure of the adversary confrontation of a press conference. But put him in front of a TV camera on a panel show, and somehow he doesn't come across as sincere and credible as he does in the flesh. Then, when he gets up on the platform once each year when he has to face the stockholders, he has some difficulty in maintaining order and control. He's much better in a one-on-one situation.

When hit with a series of crises, the president or chairman in our survey reacts most strongly to a proxy fight or any such attempt by another to acquire his company. Whether it is an automatic defense mechanism that's intrinsic to the job or whether it's the survival instinct, our chief executive treats these as threats and moves quickly into action with all the power he can muster.

Today's corporate chief has moved leftward of the stereotypical presidential posture. When questioned, the CEO generally calls himself a conservative-liberal. His associate executives see him as a liberal-conservative. But he's not a political reformer at any level—local, regional, or national.

His political activities are most often confined to donations to his party of the moment, and he gives generously. The chief executive has never run for elective office, although he urges his subordinates to seek and hold elective and appointive offices. He, himself, would rather dodge any active campaigning for any political candidate. Actually, he tries to keep his political views to himself.

Like his peers in other companies, this chief executive finds the work day and the work week too short. Often, he takes bulging cases of work home with him, and he frequently calls members of his staff at their homes at night. Not infrequently, he calls his staff together for week-end meetings. Our man isn't lazy.

It isn't only corporate work that occupies him, for although he's more likely to give some money to educational and charitable institutions, he does spot some community need and initiate action on it. He also pitches in to help solve social problems at times and will, on certain occasions, devote some of his time to civic activities. He does this primarily as a neighborhood resident with special talents. From his office, he will on occasion assign salaried people for philanthropic work at specific agencies.

Personal activities of our chief executive are taken up to a great extent by reading. Magazines top his list of reading choices, but as one might expect, it's news about business in weekly magazines. Of course, he reads the general news summaries in these weekly publications. He sort of skips over the sections in them, though, that deal with intellectual or social matters.

He's a reader of the *Wall Street Journal, New York Times* and *National Observer,* although this is often done in his office.

Our CEO gulps down a lot of books each year, about six times the national average, but not all of them are concerned with business. Fiction is his principal book fare. Perhaps the paperback mystery-detective stories act as a relief valve for him on his many necessary long flights, or they may be used as the mechanism of distraction to allow his subconscious to work out problems. In any case, he reads about twice as many works of fiction as he does books on public affairs, and about four times as many as those oriented to scientific matters.

When he's not reading, the chief executive is a great watcher of TV sports and news. Other programing generally does not interest him. He listens to the radio, either in his car or at home, to catch the latest news and sports results, too.

When he goes out for an evening's relaxation, he usually goes to the theater. Other priorities for these evenings are (in order) museums, symphony concerts and, a poor last choice, the opera.

Among the chief executive's spectator sports interests, football is number one by a wide margin. Although hockey or basketball would seem to be next choices for him, he'd rather watch a tennis match. Occasionally, he'll sit still for a baseball game, but not too often.

When it comes down to his own sports activities, the chief executive prefers golf above any other. When he got to his post at the top of his corporation, our chief executive seems to have almost entirely lost his interest in squash and handball.

He chooses fishing over hunting, but this may well be the result of environmental influences. On the water, he would rather sail than go off in a power boat. He's twice as likely to be called a "rag man" as a "stink potter." He's not often found on the ski slopes during the comparatively few free hours at his disposal.

Apparently, he'd rather stay at home and play bridge. His liking for chess as an indoor game is nil. This ties in directly with one of his traits—impatience.

The respondents to the questionnaire have been positive in their limning of a chief executive. He comes out sharp and recognizable. And quite obviously, he is a complex man, with inherent or acquired good or bad qualities that have helped him become the chief executive.

12
Will the *real* chief executive please stand up?

The answers to the questionnaire which dictated the lineaments of the portrait of the contemporary corporate chief officer have, by implication, described the next breed of presidents or chairmen who will direct the destinies of our economy.

No one can deny that tomorrow, today's chief executive will be as dead as Adam Smith.

Critics of our current crop of corporate chiefs believe that the "Establishment" has had the same attitude toward the public weal since William Vanderbilt. But change is constant. It's only the rate of change that differs, paralleling the speed of advances in technology and social sciences. From a historical perspective, transitional phases are of momentary duration, and they never cease occurring.

But what about this next breed of corporate chiefs? What can we infer from the metamorphosis? Despite his being an innovator—whereas his predecessor abhorred wave-making—the new chief executive will have difficulty in breaking cleanly away from older approaches on major issues. This new CEO will be like the military brass who fight the next war the way they fought the one they just finished.

Our new president or chairman (chairperson) may well be a woman, since more and more is there recognition of top managerial qualities of women. Sex has no mortgage on the summit.

131

The upcoming corporate chief will probably be younger —under 45—as more early retirements are taken. Another factor which indicates more youthful chiefs is the increasing tempo and variety of decision-making and its required resilience. As one senior executive put it, "Getting up for crises and problems is much tougher for older men."

Our new CEO's education will be sharpened to a finer focus. No longer will a standard master's degree in business administration be adequate. The new chief executive will probably have been educated through the broader-gauged "schools of management" rather than the "B" schools. (And the schools have shown recognition and response to this.)

The new chief executive will concentrate more on such things as the social and political environment and the continuing need to adjust to changes in human expectations and societal values. The CEO will hone his or her communication skills through new training in them. The new breed of corporate chiefs will take more advantage of new uses of computers, and having become literate in computerese, will utilize them in business or economic "war games" or problem simulations, applying a dynamism to this that was lacking previously. Yet the CEO will also be aware that computers, no matter how advanced and complex, are still electronic devices and as such have limits. So the new corporate chief will be flexible enough to know when to go away from them and when to go one-on-one when the occasion demands the sensitivity that only a human can impart.

Because of this flexibility (opportunity-orientation, if you will), our CEO will be more cognizant of more kinds of things and will, consequently, search for, employ, and assign a higher calibre of subordinate executives to handle "routine" work.

The corporate chief of the future will have supplemented a generalist education and training by getting a pragmatic knowledge of other styles of thought and other areas of activity. This person will have deliberately chosen and worked, for comparatively short periods, at a variety of tasks and assignments in a number of different organizations. Thus, the CEO will have picked up invaluable "front-line" experience and exposure to more of the publics with whom he or she will be dealing later. The new CEO will have become considerably more efficient as a communicator than are today's corporate heads.

Like a politician, tomorrow's CEO will do more "base touching" or "fence mending" with various constituencies and will also have significantly less privacy than was enjoyed by past presidents or chairmen. There will be more demands on the CEO's family. The CEO's spouse will have more to say and will be more of a partner. Hence, the CEO's family, too, must be trained to meet these new demands.

Management is still moving up the forward limb of the learning curve. Money alone will no longer be enough to satisfy our new chief executive's desires or hungers to stretch managerial muscles.

In line with being a more public person, the new chief executive will take more sabbatical leaves, putting in time as a lecturer at universities or taking on assignments for government missions or task forces.

At the local level, the corporate chief will be more of a participant. The CEO will become more active by using his or her expertise to help to solve community problems instead of just appearing among a roster of sponsors on letterheads.

Tomorrow's corporate chief will increasingly become a moderator, getting higher-calibre subordinates and delegating more of the routine chief executive's tasks to them. However, the CEO will be more reluctant to accept compromise, rejecting, as moderator, the traditional double standards of business.

This chief executive will equate, in importance, the preservation and more efficient utilization of natural resources with inflation and energy crises. The corporate chief will pay more attention to the need for, and the implementation of, political reform and improvement of the social order.

As changes come about, the CEO can expect more crises, but will be able to cope with them better than did chief executives of the past. The new CEO will be younger, have better reflexes, be more flexible and resilient, and be trained specifically for confrontation. Also, the corporate chief will use tactical forces more in combating unexpected contingencies.

Having recognized communications as a primary tool for chief executives and having been educated and trained in these skills, the new CEO will be a better speaker, better prepared to handle the problems peculiar to stockholder meetings. Personal appearances, as well as more frequent TV appearances will reveal the CEO as highly personable, starkly candid, sincere, and empathetic. The CEO will not look aloof or cold, but will reveal a human with a wide range of knowledge and skills.

Such corporate chiefs will eventually improve the public attitude toward business in general. As this change comes about, it would not be surprising to find this new type of top managers being drafted as candidates for national office. Their training is implicit in their successful operation as chief executives.

In common with their predecessors, the new corporate chiefs will take work home at night and on week-ends. But unlike the presidents or chairmen of the past, tomorrow's top executives will be "rounder" persons, finding time and having the desire to enjoy the arts more often and more wholeheartedly. They will read more, too. (The general public is trending that way.)

Younger than those corporate chiefs of the prior generation, the new breed will be more active in physical sports. Watching will give way to participating. Interest in playing "war games" will extend to chess and some of the newer intellectual exercises.

On the home front, the next group of chief executives, because of early retirement, will have more need for owning second homes and perhaps a third, special-purpose habitations, i.e., ski lodges, fishing camps, *pieds-à-terres* in other frequently visited countries or cities.

We can anticipate that the new chief executive will be more likely to have more than one marriage (as is the case with today's chief executive). There's a trend, too, indicating that the new CEO will have fewer than the 2.87 children averaged by today's corporate chief.

Because of their increased sensitivity to the societal aspects of our civilization, the new, young chief executives will be less likely to have a political label. But if they do, it will be "liberal" —with a dash of "conservative."

In comparison with the immediate past generation of chief executives, the new ones will differ markedly in a number of personal qualities. For instance, the new corporate chiefs will want to, and will, in fact, get along better with peers, superiors, and subordinates. They'll be more innovative, articulate, and communicative. They will be more curious and ingenious, and their powers of concentration will be more acute. Their boldness, displayed as innovativeness, will surpass that of their predecessors.

Like earlier chief executives, the new ones will have a high degree of integrity; will be achievement-oriented; will accept responsibility, not only for their own actions and decisions, but also for those to whom they have delegated authority. Obviously normal qualities attendant on becoming chief executive —leadership, loyalty, and drive—they will have in normal measure.

Naturally, the next generation of presidents or chairmen will also have negative traits, but they will be fewer than are found in the present generation. The new corporate chiefs will not be as arrogant, autocratic, or dictatorial. They'll be less secretive or close-mouthed and not at all nepotistic. But they will be like their predecessors in impatience and intolerance. However, this intolerance will be of bad judgment, not of failure. The new breed will be more likely to face up to issues, since it will be a tenet of the new generation not to shirk confrontation.

The next chief executives will be aware of the cumulative effect of the seemingly irrelevant, minor decisions they made earlier in their careers. They will know that success (or failure) will probably never result from a single, dramatic decision. Rather, it is the conditioning and tempering of all prior decisions which, coming together like the ingredients of a bouillabaisse, suddenly produce or reveal the final, whole product.

Unlike corporate chiefs of the past, the new chiefs will assume the public nature of their role. They will recognize the "bigness" factor—the bigger the company, the more exposed, and hence more vulnerable, it is. They will be sensitive, too, to the importance that the concerned publics attach to the postures and activities of large corporations; they will know that this sometimes erroneous importance grows exponentially with increasing size.

That we shall have such a breed of chief executives cannot be in doubt. The contemporary president or chairman is as obsolete as his stereotype. And if our relationship to one another, to shelter and food, to survival rests on the primordial law of supply and demand, we are certain that there is now a clamoring demand for a superior chief executive.

If such a corporate head had not evolved, one would have to be invented. In any case, the demand will be satisfied.

V

Q&A

13
Questionnaire and Tabulation

1. a) Do you report directly to the president of your company?

	Number	Percent
Yes	129	54.2
No	104	43.7
No answer	2	0.8
Other	3	1.3
Total	238	100.0

Note: Eleven respondents who answered "No" stated that they report to the chairman of the board and chief executive officer. If the question had read: "Do you report directly to the chief executive officer of your company?" the responses would be: "Yes"—140 (58.8%); "No"—93 (39.1%).

b) How long have you been directing the public relations activities of your company?

	Number	Percent
25 years or more	4	1.7
21–24 years	13	5.5
15–19 years	19	8.0
10–14 years	40	16.8
5–9 years	66	27.7
Under 5 years	96	40.3
Total	238	100.0

c) What are your own chances of ever becoming president of the company?

	Number	Percent
Excellent	4	1.7
Better than average	11	4.6
Average	21	8.8
Lower than average	51	21.4
None	145	60.9
No answer	2	0.8
Other	4	1.7
Total	238	99.9

2. Which of these statements best describes the president's involvement in writing the speeches he delivers?

	Number	Percent
Writes all or most of his own speeches	36	15.1
Writes his own draft and asks you to edit/rewrite	48	20.2
Asks you for a draft and then submits it to other executives	48	20.2
Tells you what to write, but makes major changes	41	17.2
Asks a number of executives for drafts	9	3.8
Tells you what to write and seldom changes your draft	61	25.6
No answer	4	1.7
Other	19	8.0
Total	266*	111.8†

*Some respondents checked more than one answer.
†Adds up to more than 100% because of multiple answers.

3. Which of the following outside inquiries does the president tend to handle personally?

	Number	Percent
Security analyst asking about financial condition of company	91	38.2
Union official seeking views on up-coming negotiations	32	13.4
Congressman seeking views on a public issue Official of environmental protection agency seeking company views on air and water pollution standards	111	46.6
	35	14.7
Spokesman for consumer protection group seeking explanation for undesirable company practices	30	12.6
Reporter or writer of national or local importance seeking information about company stand on public issue	94	39.5
None	22	9.2
No answer	27	11.3
Other	2	0.8
Total	444	186.3*

*Percentage adds up to more than 100% because some respondents checked more than one answer.

4. In which of the following areas is your president strongest? (Please rank by using a "1" for the strongest area, a "2" for the next strongest area, etc.)

	Marketing			Financial	
Rank	Number	Percent	Rank	Number	Percent
1	40	17	1	58	24
2	32	14	2	43	19
3	25	13	3	35	19
4	24	14	4	21	12
5	22	14	5	18	12
6	15	9	6	9	7
7	13	10	7	6	4
8	5	4	8	1	1

4. (cont.)

	Legal			Scientific/Technical	
Rank	Number	Percent	Rank	Number	Percent
1	13	5	1	17	7
2	10	4	2	15	7
3	10	5	3	10	4
4	17	10	4	16	10
5	14	9	5	16	10
6	23	16	6	12	8
7	39	29	7	18	14
8	34	26	8	43	33

	Production			General management	
Rank	Number	Percent	Rank	Number	Percent
1	13	5	1	92	38
2	23	10	2	64	27
3	27	14	3	28	15
4	22	12	4	12	7
5	23	15	5	3	2
6	26	18	6	3	3
7	12	9	7	1	1
8	7	6	8	1	1

	Public relations			Employee/Labor relations	
Rank	Number	Percent	Rank	Number	Percent
1	8	3	1	1	1
2	15	15	2	8	4
3	33	18	3	22	12
4	39	23	4	22	12
5	24	16	5	34	22
6	26	18	6	30	21
7	19	14	7	25	19
8	17	13	8	21	16

5. Beyond his responsibility to his stockholders to make a profit, which of the following additional responsibilities does your president accept?

	Completely No.	(%)	Partly No.	(%)	Not at all No.	(%)	No answer No.	(%)	Other No.	(%)
a) To make financial contributions to educational and charitable institutions	94	(39.1)	119	(49.6)	16	(6.3)	7	(2.9)	2	(0.8)
b) To provide salaried personnel for philanthropic work	38	(16.0)	127	(53.4)	58	(24.4)	11	(4.6)	4	(1.7)
c) To help solve social problems	49	(20.6)	148	(62.2)	30	(12.6)	8	(3.4)	3	(1.3)
d) To devote his time to civic activities	59	(24.8)	134	(56.3)	38	(16.0)	5	(2.1)	2	(0.8)
e) To initiate action in response to community needs	56	(23.5)	125	(52.5)	43	(18.1)	13	(5.5)	1	(0.4)

6. How high a priority would your president assign to each of the following social problems?

	Very high No. (%)	High No. (%)	Medium No. (%)	Low No. (%)	Very low No. (%)	No answer No. (%)	Don't know No. (%)	Other No. (%)
a) Inflation	125 (52.1)	85 (35.7)	17 (7.1)	6 (2.5)	1 (0.4)	4 (1.7)		
b) Energy crisis	156 (65.5)	63 (26.5)	12 (5.0)	4 (1.7)	1 (0.4)	2 (0.8)		
c) International monetary and trade arrangements	77 (32.4)	67 (28.2)	58 (24.4)	20 (8.4)	10 (4.2)	6 (2.5)		1 (0.4)
d) Tax reform	45 (18.9)	91 (38.2)	69 (29.0)	19 (8.0)	7 (2.9)	6 (2.5)		
e) Education	28 (11.8)	81 (34.0)	81 (34.0)	37 (15.5)	6 (2.5)	5 (2.1)		
f) Air and water pollution	57 (23.9)	75 (31.5)	72 (30.3)	22 (9.2)	4 (1.7)	4 (1.7)		4 (1.7)
g) Employment of minorities and disadvantaged	49 (20.6)	71 (29.8)	85 (35.7)	18 (7.6)	8 (3.4)	5 (2.1)		2 (0.8)
h) Community development	29 (12.2)	71 (29.8)	85 (35.7)	37 (15.5)	11 (4.6)	3 (1.3)		2 (0.8)
i) Preserving natural resources	27 (11.3)	66 (27.7)	99 (41.6)	28 (11.8)	11 (4.6)	7 (2.9)		
j) Political reform at local, state, and national levels	17 (7.1)	57 (23.9)	82 (34.5)	53 (22.3)	21 (8.8)	7 (2.9)	1 (0.4)	
k) Fair and equal job opportunities	67 (28.2)	79 (33.2)	70 (29.4)	16 (6.7)	3 (1.3)	3 (1.3)		
l) Stabilization of social order	23 (9.7)	58 (24.4)	87 (36.6)	37 (15.5)	22 (9.2)	7 (2.9)	3 (1.3)	1 (0.4)

7. What is your president's most typical reaction in the face of
the following situations?

		Number	Percent
a)	Proxy fight:		
	Treats as major crisis	90	37.8
	Shows extreme concern	33	13.9
	Becomes totally preoccupied	7	2.9
	Applies standard operating procedure	27	11.3
	Shrugs off to subordinates	3	1.3
	Treats casually	9	3.8
	Never experienced	9	3.8
	Not applicable	21	8.8
	Don't know	3	1.3
	No answer	36	15.1
			100.0
b)	Acquisition or tender offer:		
	Treats as major crisis	72	30.3
	Shows extreme concern	54	23.0
	Becomes totally preoccupied	12	5.0
	Applies standard operating procedure	31	13.0
	Shrugs off to subordinates	3	1.3
	Treats casually	7	2.9
	Never experienced	8	3.4
	Not applicable	17	7.1
	Don't know	2	0.8
	No answer	32	13.4
			100.2
c)	Demonstration by social protest group:		
	Treats as major crisis	8	3.4
	Shows extreme concern	55	23.1
	Becomes totally preoccupied	13	5.5
	Applies standard operating procedure	97	40.8
	Shrugs off to subordinates	26	10.9
	Treats casually	9	3.8
	Other	11	4.6
	No answer	19	8.0
			100.1

7. (Cont.)

		Number	Percent
d)	Appearing as witness at legislative or public hearing:		
	Treats as major crisis	9	3.8
	Shows extreme concern	71	29.8
	Becomes totally preoccupied	25	10.5
	Applies standard operating procedure	95	39.9
	Shrugs off to subordinates	14	5.9
	Treats casually	8	3.4
	Other	4	1.7
	No answer	12	5.0
			100.0
e)	Labor ultimatum:		
	Treats as major crisis	22	9.2
	Shows extreme concern	52	21.8
	Becomes totally preoccupied	13	5.5
	Applies standard operating procedure	107	45.0
	Shrugs off to subordinates	16	6.7
	Treats casually	1	0.4
	Other	5	2.1
	No answer	22	9.2
			99.9
f)	Hostile press:		
	Treats as major crisis	18	7.6
	Shows extreme concern	80	33.6
	Becomes totally preoccupied	13	5.5
	Applies standard operating procedure	73	30.7
	Shrugs off to subordinates	25	10.5
	Treats casually	13	5.5
	Other	5	2.1
	Don't know	1	0.4
	No answer	10	4.2
			100.1

7. (Cont.)

		Number	Percent
g)	Condemnation by FTC, FDA, SEC, or other governmental agency:		
	Treats as major crisis	48	20.2
	Shows extreme concern	98	41.2
	Becomes totally preoccupied	15	6.3
	Applies standard operating procedure	53	22.3
	Shrugs off to subordinates	3	1.3
	Treats casually	2	0.8
	Other	6	2.5
	No answer	13	5.5
			100.1
h)	Extraordinary or unexpected happenings/ events:		
	Treats as major crisis	21	8.8
	Shows extreme concern	72	30.3
	Becomes totally preoccupied	24	10.1
	Applies standard operating procedure	95	39.9
	Shrugs off to subordinates	3	1.3
	Treats casually	6	2.9
	Other	7	2.5
	Don't know	3	1.3
	No answer	7	2.9
			100.0

8. How high or low would you rate your president on the following communication skills?

	Excellent No. (%)	High No. (%)	Medium No. (%)	Low No. (%)	Poor No. (%)	No answer No. (%)	Don't know No.(%)	Other No. (%)
a) Hear and absorb oral presentations	163 (68.5)	60 (25.2)	10 (4.2)	5 (2.1)	0			
b) Absorb/understand written material	162 (68.1)	64 (26.9)	10 (4.2)	2 (0.8)	0			
c) Is sensitive to between-the-line messages	101 (42.4)	81 (34.0)	40 (16.8)	11 (4.6)	2 (0.8)	3 (1.3)		
d) Conduct productive group meetings	70 (29.4)	86 (36.1)	62 (26.1)	13 (5.5)	2 (0.8)	5 (2.1)		
e) Speak effectively in public	79 (33.2)	66 (27.7)	73 (30.7)	14 (5.9)	5 (2.1)	1 (0.4)		
f) Appear truthful and candid at press conferences	140 (58.8)	71 (29.8)	22 (9.2)	3 (1.3)	0	2 (0.8)		
g) Listen attentively and exercise control in "eyeball" confrontations	102 (42.9)	91 (38.2)	31 (13.0)	11 (4.6)	2 (0.8)	1 (0.4)		
h) Come across as sincere and credible in television appearances	82 (34.5)	84 (35.3)	44 (18.5)	7 (2.9)		14 (5.9)	5 (2.1)	2 (0.8)
i) Maintain order at stockholder meetings	119 (50.0)	76 (31.9)	17 (7.1)	1 (0.4)	0	15 (6.3)		10 (4.2)

9. Which of these activities and attitudes describe your president's involvement in politics? (Check those statements that apply to him.)

	Number	Percent
Has run for office on national level	0	
Has run for office on state or local level	9	3.8
Urges other executives to hold elective or appointive office	52	21.8
Has held an appointed office in government	38	16.0
Has actively campaigned for political candidates	33	13.9
Has given generously to political party of his choice	121	50.8
Airs his political views in public	59	24.8
Keeps his political views private	152	63.9
No answer	4	1.7
Other	2	0.8
Total	470	197.5*

*Percentage column adds up to more than 100% because of multiple mentions by some respondents.

10. Which of the following activities describes your president?

	Often	Sometimes	Never	No answer	Don't know	Other
a) Takes work home with him	155 (65.1)	68 (28.6)	10 (4.2)	4 (1.7)	1 (0.4)	
b) Telephones subordinates at all hours of the night	15 (6.3)	113 (47.5)	96 (40.3)	9 (3.8)	2 (0.8)	3 (1.3)
c) Holds weekend meetings with staff members	27 (11.3)	114 (47.9)	84 (35.3)	10 (4.2)	1 (0.4)	2 (0.8)
d) Attends:						
(1) opera	36 (15.1)	74 (31.1)	46 (19.3)	75 (31.5)	6 (2.5)	1 (0.4)
(2) symphony	47 (19.7)	94 (39.5)	35 (14.7)	55 (23.1)	6 (2.5)	1 (0.4)
(3) theater	67 (28.2)	122 (51.3)	18 (7.6)	26 (10.9)	4 (1.7)	1 (0.4)
(4) museums	47 (19.7)	93 (39.1)	31 (13.0)	60 (25.2)	6 (2.5)	1 (0.4)
e) Watches television:						
(1) sports	95 (39.9)	89 (37.4)	12 (5.0)	37 (15.5)	5 (2.1)	
(2) news	156 (65.5)	59 (24.8)	1 (0.4)	17 (7.1)	5 (2.1)	
(3) other	38 (16.0)	106 (44.5)	9 (3.8)	78 (32.8)	6 (2.5)	1 (0.4)
f) Listens to radio:						
(1) sports	39 (16.4)	77 (32.4)	31 (13.0)	81 (34.0)	9 (3.8)	1 (0.4)
(2) news	90 (37.8)	96 (40.3)	5 (2.1)	35 (14.7)	11 (4.6)	1 (0.4)
(3) other	33 (13.9)	81 (34.0)	22 (9.2)	94 (39.5)	7 (2.9)	1 (0.4)
g) Reads national newspapers	199 (83.6)	25 (10.5)	2 (0.8)	10 (4.2)	2 (0.8)	
h) Reads magazines dealing with:						
(1) weekly news	203 (85.3)	24 (10.1)	0	9 (3.8)	2 (0.8)	
(2) business	214 (90.0)	12 (5.0)	0	10 (4.2)	2 (0.8)	
(3) intellectual/social matters	85 (35.7)	97 (40.8)	18 (7.6)	35 (14.7)	3 (1.3)	
i) Combines business with vacation trips	97 (40.8)	108 (45.4)	22 (9.2)	8 (3.4)	2 (0.8)	1 (0.4)

10. (Cont.)

j) About how many books a year does he read dealing with:

	Public affairs	Business & economics	Behavioral science	Scientific matters	Fiction
Number of books: 0	8	6	17	32	18
1	22	12	27	12	4
2	26	23	17	12	11
3	14	13	4	4	10
4	5	14	3	5	5
5	13	8	7	6	9
6	6	15	0	2	11
7	0	2	1	0	0
8	2	1	0	0	1
10	4	12	5	3	6
12	1	2	0	0	1
15	1	1	0	0	1
20	2	1	0	0	5
25	0	0	0	0	1
30	0	1	0	0	0
40	1	1	0	0	0
Average:	3.9	5.2	2.2	1.8	5.0
No answer:	62.0	47.0	80.0	81.0	68.0
Don't know:	69.0	68.0	73.0	73.0	78.0
Other:	7.0	12.0	6.0	5.0	9.0

k) His favorite recreational activities are: (Check as many as apply.)

	No. (%)		No. (%)
Golf	133 (55.9)	Squash	11 (4.6)
Tennis	72 (30.3)	Skiing	43 (18.0)
Sailing	51 (21.4)	Chess	4 (1.7)
Power boating	27 (11.3)	Bridge	31 (13.0)
Fishing	49 (20.6)	None	3 (1.3)
Hunting	39 (16.4)	No answer	15 (6.3)
Handball	4 (1.7)	Other	15 (6.3)

10. (Cont.)

1) His favorite spectator sports
are: (Check as many as apply.)

Baseball	41 (17.2)
Football	149 (62.6)
Hockey	32 (13.4)
Basketball	32 (13.4)
Tennis matches	52 (21.8)
Swim meets	7 (2.9)
None	2 (0.8)
No answer	44 (18.5)
Don't know	7 (2.9)

m) Does he own a second home?

Yes	135 (56.7)
No	93 (39.1)
No answer	10 (4.2)

n) Does he attend church?

Yes	159 (66.8)
No	46 (19.3)
No answer	26 (10.9)
Don't know	7 (2.9)

o) Has he been married?

Once	209 (87.8)
Twice	20 (8.4)
More than twice	4 (1.7)
Never	2 (0.8)
No answer	3 (1.3)

10. (Cont.)

p) How many children does he have (average, 2.87)?

	Number	(%)
0	7	2.9
1	17	7.1
2	76	31.9
3	64	26.9
4	36	15.1
5	10	4.2
6	10	4.2
7	4	1.7
No answer	14	5.8
	238	99.8

q) How old is he?

Under 35	2	0.8
35–44	21	8.8
45–54	104	43.7
55–65	104	43.7
Over 65	4	1.7
No answer	3	1.3
	238	100.0

r) His political orientation is:

Conservative	98	40.8
Liberal conservative	61	25.6
Conservative-liberal	58	24.4
Liberal	15	6.3
Progressive	2	0.8
Other	1	0.4
No answer	7	2.9
	242	101.2*

*Some respondents checked more than one political orientation.

10. (Cont.)

s) What type of car does he own?

	Number	(%)
Luxury	137	57.1
Sports	16	6.7
Foreign	38	16.0
Standard	75	31.5
None	3	1.3
No answer	4	1.7
	273	114.3*

*Some company presidents and chairmen own more than one car.

11. Which five of the following qualities does your president consider pivotal when he hires an executive? (Check five items.)

	No.	(%)		No.	(%)
Achievement orientation	105	44.1	Concentration	10	4.2
Initiative	103	43.3	Articulateness	24	10.1
Integrity	121	50.8	Imagination	24	10.1
Getting along with peers	19	8.0	Curiosity	3	1.3
			Enthusiasm	54	22.7
Getting along with superiors	12	5.0	Communicativeness	31	13.0
Getting along with subordinates	11	4.6	Ingenuity	16	6.7
			Drive	67	28.2
Prudence	14	5.9	Loyalty	70	29.4
Creativity	55	23.1	No answer	11	4.6
Leadership	95	40.0	Don't know	3	1.3
Acceptance of responsibility	117	49.2	Other	1	0.4
Reliability	99	41.6			
Boldness	14	5.9			
Perception	44	18.5			

12. Which of these traits could in any way be applied to your president? (Check all relevant traits.)

	No.	(%)		No.	(%)
Secretive	25	10.5	Impersonal and		
Close-mouthed	57	23.9	unemotional	46	19.3
Nepotistic	17	7.1	Arrogant	15	6.3
Egotistic	53	22.3	Impatient	79	33.2
Opinionated	77	32.4	Autocratic and		
Intolerant of	63	26.5	dictatorial	42	17.6
failure			Issue avoidance	26	10.9
Cold and objective	35	14.7	None	16	6.7
			No answer	42	17.6